Zen

and Modern Consciousness

Scott Shaw

BUDDHA ROSE PUBLICATIONS

Zen and Modern Consciousness
Copyright © 2011 by Scott Shaw
All Rights Reserved.
www.scottshaw.com

Rear cover photographs of Scott Shaw by
Hae Won Shin
Copyright © 2011 All Rights Reserved.

No part of this book may be reproduced in any manner without the expressed written permission of the author or the publishing Company.

First Edition

ISBN: 1-877792-52-7
ISBN 13: 9781877792526

Library of Congress Control Number: 2011924528

10 9 8 7 6 5 4 3 2 1

Printed in the United States of America

ZEN
and Modern Consciousness

Contents

	Introduction	9
1	Giving	13
2	Judgment	25
3	Evolution	33
4	Human Nature	41
5	Are Your Forgiven?	49
6	The Silence of Mind	59
7	Planned Parenthood	65
8	Getting What You Want	69
9	A Position of Authority	79
10	You Are Not a Christian	91
11	The Emotion of Emotion	101
12	The Rules Are For Sissies	111
13	They Love You and They Hate You	117

14	What's the Point of Reading Book?	123
15	It Takes Two to Tango: Conflict on the Spiritual Path	129
16	No One Wants Success They Just Want to Know How Much They Are Getting Paid	155
17	Paying For Your Sins	163
18	Analyzing the Moments	173
19	Reviewing the Life and the Works of Others	177
20	Interpretation	183
21	Things You Will Never Know	191
22	In Your Own Moment	199
	About the Author	205
	Scott Shaw *Books-in-Print*	207

Introduction

Zen is much more than a philosophic and religious school of thought attributed to Buddhism.

Zen is much more than siting and meditating.

Zen is a universal consciousness where an individual is allowed to tune into a mindset where they can consciously interact with universal knowledge and supreme understanding. They do this while still maintaining their grasp of physical reality and their interaction with the material world.

Zen is not abstract, though it is illusive. Zen is not a lack of reality. It is a supreme, absolute, reality.

Zen is everyday and everything. Though many, who do not understand the true essence of Zen, attempt to hide it behind a veil of illusion. But, the hidden has nothing to do with Zen.

Zen is here. Zen is now. Zen is you.

To embrace Zen, all you must do is to give into Zen. Meaning, you must let go and know.

Because, in fact, and in reality, you already know. You know that you know. You may just have forgotten this fact.

In the pages of this book, we will discus Zen and its interaction with common, everyday, physical reality. For this is the reality that we, as human beings, must embrace, live through, and learn from, each day.

As the physical body and the thinking mind are both equal parts that define us as human beings -- from reading the pages of this book it is hoped that you will gain some insight into how to more consciously interact with and learn from your thoughts and why you think them; your physical actions and why your perform them; your interactions with others and how you meet other people and interplay with them in this place we call life.

It is hoped that from the insight you may gain from this book that, perhaps, the next time you encounter a new set of life circumstances or relive old ones, you will be better prepared to pass through the process and evolve into a more refined mindset instead of becoming trapped in the constraints of everyday physical resistance. …You will be able to embody Zen as opposed to being dominated by the ways of the world.

Embrace the Zen. Feel the perfection. And, move on, consciously through your life…

Giving

Central to the spiritual path is the concept of giving. But, giving can mean many different things to many different people. Just what is giving?

Karma Yoga
In India the concept of karma yoga was developed. In essence, karma yoga is defined as selfless service performed in order to help your teacher, your organization, a particular person, or the world at large. The primary premise behind karma yoga is that you are doing what you are doing to help someone or something, but expecting no results from your actions.

This concept, though very pure in its definition, has led to many a misconception. First of all, as defined in the definition of karma yoga itself, you are doing something and expecting nothing. Yet, in karma yoga you are told you will receive good karma for your actions. Isn't good karma a something? Though this is a very finite point, the spiritual path is riddled with these finite points and they all must be uncovered for the aspirant to enter into a state of True Knowledge.

Therefore, to understand the true essence of, *"Giving,"* you have to ask yourself, *"Why do people do anything?"* The answer is, because they expect some response or result from their actions - even if they claim this not the case. Whether these results are something concrete or something so subtle as simply being made to feel good about themselves for doing or giving something, the outcome is the same; they have done what they have done for an expected outcome.

Now, this does not necessarily diminish their actions. But, it does make the concept of giving a response-motivated action.

But, back to the premise of karma yoga...

In eastern philosophy based spiritual groups, a devotee is often guided to perform very specific actions. They are told this is for the betterment of the group or the guru. As such, it is karma yoga. In many cases the disciple does not want to the action at all. In these cases, they are told that this is truly spiritual practice and the essence of the spiritual path -- doing something that you don't want to do.

Interesting justification, don't you think? And, a great way to get people to do things that may be against their psychological or moral make-up.

Though it is not discussed, people in spiritual circles perform these actions, (their giving), to become more closely linked with the sect, the teacher, or to be seen as truly spiritual. They perform these guided actions to become a more accepted part of the communal whole. They do this in order to gain a closeness to a the group or individualize acceptance and love from a specific individual or individuals in order to fulfill whatever is lacking from the relationship aspect of their life.

Think about it, how many actions have you performed in your life to be liked, loved, and accepted by a single person or to become a part of a specific group?

From a more worldly perspective, people do things; particularly donate money, to appear as if they are a truly giving and caring person. From this they gain hoped for acceptance and self-worth.

Even from a self-help perspective, teachings have arisen that state if you give this amount of money or that amount of time, it will crate great financial results in your life. But, none of the examples actually embrace a true sense of helping and giving.
The Spiritual Path

With the true essence of the reasons for giving defined, it must be understood that the spiritual path is a funny playground. Why? Because there is all of these subtle elements of consciousness that are going on that the outsider and the spiritual novice do not understand. The spiritual path is populated by people who have heard of what this path has to offer: community, fulfillment, a calmer mind, enlightenment, god, etc. So, people step into this playground expecting to receive all of the promised benefits. And, if one does not look too deeply, they will find what they are promised.

What I always say about life, however, is that for everything you do, there is always a price to pay. And, this too is the case with the spiritual path.

On the spiritual path you will be asked to give. Now this request may come in various fashions depending on what type of sect you associate with. Christian churches commonly expect a weekly donation at the end of the service. Other religious may ask for donations or for you to provide various types of physical help to expand the cause. At its root, I suppose there is nothing wrong with any of these requests. If you have the money or the physical ability, why not help out? But here is where the slippery slope begins...

As much as most will deny this fact, people who enter the spiritual path expect something in return. If they give their time, their money, or themselves, they expect the promised community, enlightenment, god, or whatever. They want to be accepted into the fold and be given what has been promised. From this arises all of the denials commonly given on the spiritual path to those aspirants who have not achieved what they expected. *"Oh, you must meditate longer to become enlightened." "You are pure enough to personally speak with the guru." "You have to walk this path for many years and do all of the things we ask before we can award you that title or rank."* And perhaps most damning of all of the spiritual denials is, *"You must pay this amount of money and take this course if you want to progress."*

People believe all of these things. They continue to give all that the can - that is until they see through the illusion. Then, they become disillusioned and walk away from the path, nun-the-better for all of the giving that they have given. And, often times, leave having become very bitter.

The reality is, any spiritual group is out for one thing -- the group. As a collective whole, they believe what they have been taught by their teacher. From these accepted teachings, the upper echelon of the group does whatever it takes to maintain their positioning in the hierarchy of the group and to help the group to grow and expand so their beliefs are spread to more and more people and their high standing relationship with the group may be observed and honored by others. How do they do this, by asking others to give? And, what are the people who are doing the asking achieving? Nothing but feeding their own ego.

You must understand that spiritual groups are not there for you. They are in place for the dissemination of the knowledge taught by the leader of the group. If all you want is to receive, and not question a specific set of teachings, then all if fine. But, be prepared to give for what you receive and do not ask them for anything in return.
Questioning

Throughout history, man (and woman) has questioned authority. This is what has set all revolutions in motion: political, spiritual, and otherwise. But, question a spiritual group and you are shown the door. Though they may escort you to it very kindly.

Ask a spiritual group to give you something physically specific, (other than the promised abstract benefits of spiritually), you will be told, *"No."* If you contest and say, *"But I gave the church this or that."* All that will happen is that they will tell you that is the way it is suppose to be -- your giving to the church. If you continue to contest, you too will be shown the door.

I could provide you with a long list of personally witness examples of this style of behavior on the part of religious based sects -- some even made the news. But, I believe that we have all heard of these circumstances occurring, so it is unnecessary.

On the other side of the coin, believe the teachings, ask for nothing, be prepared to give all that is asked of you, and all is well -- you may remain a content member of the group.

Giving

So then, what is giving and why should you give?

Giving must be based in what you have to offer and what you are willing to discard.

So many times I have walked down the street and a homeless person is asking for change and a person will tell them, *"Get a job."* Or, *"All you will use the money for is drugs or alcohol."* Or if they have a pet dog with them, *"Why don't you just eat your dog."* But, what is the negative emotion base on. It is based in the self-righteous attitude of the person who is spewing these words.

Maybe the person would get a job if they could. Maybe they will use the money for drugs or alcohol. But, why would anyone want to eat their best friend?

None of these responses have anything to do with giving. All they have to with is ego. But, we all have to realize how fast everything we call, *"Known,"* can be taken from us by an untold number of catastrophic circumstances. That is the cornerstone of life. We never know what is around the next turn. So, if you can give to a person asking for something, (if you want to give to a person asking for something), then give. But, if you do not want to, berating them does nothing but bring you bad energy. So, just tell the person that you can't help them out right now and walk on.

Like I always suggest, if you are going to be homeless (or crazy) move to India, because there, instead of simply being a bum, you will be considered holy and the society will take care of you.

Here lies the essence of the cultural differences about giving. In India, if you are a homeless person, a sadhu, you are a saint.

People believe that they generate good karma by feeding and taking care of you. In the west, if you are homeless, you are seen as adding to an ever-growing problem, and very few people are willing to give you anything.

Who is Asking

The other side of the issue is, who is asking for you to give and why.

Here in California it is very common for a person to come up to you at a gas station or a parking lot and tell you that they ran out of gas and they need money to buy gas to get back to their family or to buy a bus ticket to get to their sick grandmother, or whatever. In fact, when we were filming one of my movies, *The Rock n' Roll Cops,* at Los Angeles Union Station, a person using this line came up to us. Instead of just saying, *"No."* We had him perform his whole speal to two of the cast members. We filmed it and integrated it into the movie. Then we gave him some money.

But, in most cases, it is simply the job of this type of person to ask you to give them money. So, that is probably the kind of person you do not want to give to.

This situation occurred to me another time a few months ago in the affluent neighborhood of Newport Beach. California.

I was in a gas station and a guy wearing very expensive clothing came up to me and asked me for money because he ran out of gas. I smilingly told him I could not help him out. As I was pumping my gas, I noticed that he had gone into the gas station's market and paid for a cup of coffee. I smiled.

Another example of this situation happened to me today. A very down and out guy came up to me in a gas station, in South-central L.A., with a gas can. He asked for my help and I was happy to fill it for him.

On the other side of the issue, when I tried to give something to somebody, and was declined, took place in Varanasi, India. I was buying some prayer beads from a man who strung them for a living and sold them near the River Ganges. I made my selection and he told me the price of two rupees. Trying to be nice and GIVE, I handed him a one hundred-rupee note. But, he would have nothing to do with it. All he would accept was his stated price of two rupees.

This is an essential lesson to learn about giving. Most people ask for it. Few, the truly whole and spiritual, refuse it. So, ultimately, you give what you can, when you can. You must keep your eyes open to who you give to, because if you do not you will give and you may be left feeling taken advantage of -- lord knows I (like many others) have felt that way several times in my life. But, if you give simply to give, then it does not matter what the person or group does with your gifts. All that matters is that you gave.

So, define your own parameters about giving. And, then give. Because this is what makes this place called life worth living -- helping others when you can help them. Because then they will move forward and give when they can give. From this, the world becomes a much better place.

Judgment

"I enjoy your book, About Peace. I was surprised to see the photograph that you have chosen to put on the home page of your web page. I am really disappointed that you have chosen to use women as objects to promote yourself. Please consider how offensive this is. I had considered buying more copies of your book to give as gifts, but now I am really disillusioned about who you are and what you believe and promote."

This is an e-mail that I received and it pretty much speaks for itself. What it also ideally depicts is the perceived illusion, the maya, if you will, of how people expect other people to behave. In fact, what many people desire is that other people act in a predetermined manner that they deem appropriate in accordance with their own definition of reality. Which leads me to the point of this article...

I often discuss with people how personal judgment, about another person's life and another person's choices, truly effects, in a negative manner, an individual's own life and their own interaction with life-fulfillment and enlightenment. The statement that is posted above is an ideal example of what keeps one from truly embracing all this world has to offer.

Is the above e-mail based in spirituality? No it is not. It is based in judgment. And, this is the reason that I always suggest to people that they remove themselves from all preconceived notions and never sit in judgment of another person's life.

Why? Because, in a nutshell, no outside individual can ever possess all of the facts and understanding about another person's life and why they do what they do.

But, let's continue...

Buying a Book

If a person buys one of my books and they enjoy it or it helps them, that's great. If while reading the book, they find some sense of deeper meaning and life-happiness, even better. That is why I wrote About Peace and other books on spirituality. But, you have to understand an essential fact about life, we each seek what we seek. If we are seeking spirituality, then we will find spirituality. We will travel to places where spirituality exists and we will find books like *About Peace* and other spiritual writings.

It is just the simple fact of life; we find what we are looking for.

But, now here comes the other side of the issue, when we are looking for something, we have already come to define what we consider the definition of that SOMETHING to be. If we are seeking spirituality, we have already defined in our mind what we consider spirituality to look like. As I have talked and written about many times, spirituality is quite commonly defined in very limited terms: a person must look a certain way, dress a certain way, and do certain things.

The question then arises, however, is what you define as being spiritual, true spirituality or is it simply what your thinking mind has decided spirituality should look like?

You really need to ask yourself that question, because if spirituality is only defined by what you expect it to look like, then it is not spirituality at all, it is simply mind-stuff and that is the chief causation factor for maya, illusion. And, this is the primary reason why people never truly interaction with enlightenment, (another subject I have written extensively about), because then they are bogged down with their own created illusion of what they think enlightenment is suppose to be. Thus, they never free themselves enough to truly embrace Nirvana.

Now, it is important to understand, I am not criticizing the individual who wrote me this e-mail. In fact, I find it quite amusing, because if they knew anything about me or my website they would know that I do not, 'Use women as objects to promote myself.' I just thought the photo they referenced was a fun memory and an interesting image. And, the photos on the website are in a continuous state of flux.

Believe me, I get e-mails and letters all the time, most are very nice and complimentary. But, a few, like this one, want me to change who I am and want me to behave in a manner that the author finds appropriate.

It is essential to understand, however, that an individual who writes an e-mail like this is not simply focusing all their attention upon me. They invoke this type of behavior across the board. They want everybody to be the way they want them to be. But, this is not true spirituality. And, someone invoking this style of behavior has no right to judge anybody - not if they are an ordinary person or a well-know spiritual teacher or guru. Why? Because, attempting to dominate the actions of other people is based in ego;

thinking, *"I know more than you. I know what is right, you don't."*

That mindset is not spirituality!

I mean, let's think about it; how many of us remember when churches across the U.S. where claiming that rock n' roll was the devil's music and anybody who listened to it was a sinner? How ridiculous was that? Or, remember in the 1960s and into the 1970s if you were a male with long hair you were a totally outcast and in complete opposition to all that was just and right. What a joke!

The point I am making here is the same point that I discuss in the book *About Peace* and elsewhere in my writings,

As long as you have desires, as long as you have definitions, you will never be free. Because, you will never be happy unless your definitions are met. Which they never will be. And, you will never find enlightenment, unless enlightenment meets your expectations. But, expectations have nothing to do with spirituality or enlightenment. Expectations are not true spirituality. They are simply judgment. And, judgment has nothing to do with true spirituality!

Ultimately, what you have to do is to define what you want out of life. And, as previously discussed, you will find what you are looking for.

If you are looking for someone to criticize, you can find a million reasons, in a million people, to criticize. But, if you are seeking true spirituality, then you simply allow everything and every person to be as they are.

People Are Beautiful

Let's face it, women are beautiful. Women find men beautiful. Everybody and everything is beautiful. People ARE objects (as the e-mailer stated). We are things -- moving, living, and feeling THINGS. So, yes, we are objects, if you want to call people objects. But, that does not make us lesser human beings. What makes us lesser human beings is to unleash our judgment upon the world. For that is the basis of all conflict. And, conflict has nothing to do with true spirituality.

Feel what you feel. That is the predetermined condition of life. But, you do not have to spread your own predetermined feelings upon others.

Art

How many of us enjoy truly artistic photographs or paintings of people? I do. But, do I sit there and say that a specific photograph or painting is not spiritual or is not artistic because of what the subject in the photograph is or is not wearing? No, I do not. I may like, I may not. But, that does not change the fact that I appreciate it as art.

Here is the question you must ask yourself, *"Who has the ultimate knowledge that gives them the right to judge anybody and tell them how they should live their life?"*

Do you have that ultimate knowledge?

This is Life

This is life, you must decide who and what you are going to be. Are you going to walk through life full of predetermined judgment? Or, are you going to truly understand spiritually and accept everything and everyone for what and who they are -- allowing each individual to be who they are, embracing the arts and life as they see fit?

To people who don't know me, my life may appear to be a contradiction. But, it really is not. For me, what my life is about is bridging the gap between perceived spirituality and the world. You see, this is really common sense, but many people do not understand the simple fact that you can live in the world but not be of the world. That you can walk with sinners and still be a saint. You do not have to dress a certain way. (I used to be a Swami. Think how I used to dress.) You can do what you do, have some life-fun and still be contributing to the overall good, as opposed to the overall-bad which is born out of judgment.

We all must understand that what we think is only what we think. But, do we need to tell other people what we think? No, not unless they ask. Do we need to try to influence other people to feel what we feel, do what we do? No, that is not spirituality.

Ultimately, we must learn to keep out opinions to ourselves. Because, in truth, the only one who cares about our opinions is ourselves.

Live, love, be who you are, do what you will do. Let go and be free of judgment. This is Zen

IS -- is enlightenment. This is Zen.
IS NOT -- is not enlightenment. It is not Zen.
IS or IS NOT is your choice.
Enlightenment is your choice.
Who are you going to be? It is your choice.

Evolution

We have all done good things and we have done bad things. Some of us have done more good than bad, while others have done more bad than good. But, no one is universally good or bad. It is as simple as that.

Many people do good things in order to be liked or to be viewed in a particular light in order to have their own agendas met. This is the same reason why people do bad things -- they do them so they will be seen as evil in order to become feared so that their desires will be answered.

Many people pretend to be doing good things when they are in fact doing something quite evil. While others do things that appear to be bad but ultimately their actions turn out to have created something good.

The question must be asked, *"Why do people do what they do?"*

Certainly, there is the input of biology, psychology, and sociology, that each of us, as human beings, encounter as we are going through life. We are each born with a certain personally into a family and a social environment where we learn the rudimentary facts of life. From this, we are then exposed to a socioeconomic/cultural world were we are groomed into who we will become. At each juncture of life, however, there is CHOICE. The choices that we make, as a human being, define us as who we are, how we are viewed, and the positive or negative, good or bad, impact we will make upon other people and the world.

How we get to the point where we make the choices that we make is the pathway of life evolution. This is because of the fact, with each choice that you make, you set an entirely new set of criteria in motion which will define the next choice that you will make.

Many people claim that they do not have a choice. They claim that what they have done and what they will do is and was based solely upon their placement in their particular social structure, their country, their family, the wealth they did or did not possess, or their social environment. Certainly, these are all defining factors in a person's life. But, they are not the sole factor.

An individual, from the moment they are born, are indoctrinated into a world of thought, programmed by what their parents believe, what their friends believe, and what their society believes. Think about it, *"If no one told you about religion. If no one told you about the things you are suppose to believe, then what would you believe?"*

This brings us back to the premise of CHOICE. We each have been told what to believe -- from the time of our birth forward. Some of the things we have listened to -- others we have not. This programming has come from all kinds of sources: family, friends, religious elders, and the media.

Each of these sources of programming have they, themselves, been programmed into a belief system that they did not originate, however. It must be understood that they did not create what they believe. Someone else created it, taught it to them, and they then made the choice to accept it as their own belief system. Then, they have moved forward and imparted it onto others.

Some are very fervent with their beliefs, and really try to force their belief of what one should or should not do onto others. While others, hold their beliefs quietly within themselves.

But, what is a belief? It is simply what you believe.

Does your believing in it make it right or wrong? Does your believing in it make it the absolute truth? No, it does not. It simply makes it what you believe.

This is where many of life problems arise. People believe that what they believe is some absolute knowledge that all others must adhere to. If they do not, then they are sinners, blasphemers, unholy, and wrong. In fact, belief is the cause of all war and domination.

What gives a person the power to wage war? A consensus of belief held by the powerful whom then commands their masses to inflict their belief upon others.

Throughout human history there has been those who have dominated others. They have done this by force, violence, intimidation, and also by the promise of a great and holy reward if they believe what they are told to believe and do what they are told to do. Domination is also executed in many much more subtle ways.

From this domination, religious have been born, belief systems have been cemented into human consciousness, and nations have risen. What has given birth to this ongoing process is that generation-after-generation have been programmed into believing that they must act a certain way and do certain things if they ever hope to be advanced to the upper realms of whatever social, religious, moral, or ideological code has been programmed into them. They must wear the uniform and fight for the country if they are ever to become a true man or woman and prove they are brave and strong. They must have pure and true faith and prove it by following all of the rules if they ever wish to reach the ultimate and final stage of human consciousness, enlightenment or interaction with god. Or, from a more self-serving standpoint, they must selfishly over power others, and from their own greed emerge as rich, powerful, and able to live a lavish lifestyle.

But, let's step away from all of this for a moment. What if, the untold number of generations were never promised some great reward during, and at the end of their life, if they act and behave in a pre-designated manner. What if they were simply allowed to form their own philosophies and define what it is that they really want to believe, leading to what they will ultimately do with their life? Then, would not the death and the destruction of wars been avoided? Would the people who were burned on the cross for heresy been allowed to live their lives? Would the people who gave their moneys to false profits of religion and industry been allowed to live a more sustained life? Would their not have been much less personally inflicted guilt in people life who have done things that were looked down upon by their religious group?

You see, generation-after-generation has continued to do the same thing; program each other and then make people feel wrong and ashamed if they are not following a particular belief system to its idealized end. This is especially the case for those who are at the head of the hierarchical line -- claiming they are the most devout. Inevitably it turns out that they are sinners, just like the rest of us, and then they beg for forgiveness.

What is the answer then to all of this preprogrammed, life harming, reality? The answer is you own, personal evolution, which will lead to the evolution of the entire human race.

First of all, start at the beginning. What do you believe? Next, why do you believe it -- what does it give you -- who does it make you? Then, who around you believes what you believe? And, if you changed your belief system, how would they react? Finally, who would you be if you were to let go of your belief system - what would you become? In most cases, what you would become is FREE.

People believe what they believe because it makes them SOMETHING. They hold on to their belief, good or bad, out of fear of discovering who they really are and what they true believe if all of the layers of programming were removed.

Life is like a highway. You drive onto it with your car via the onramp. You find that there are already a group of cars going in the same direction. Some are driving slower than you; some are driving faster. Some drive badly and get in your way. Others, all you see are their taillights. Some will get off to get gas, but then they will catch up to you later. But, there will be some that are driving at the same speed as you. Those, you will travel down the highway with for many miles. But eventually, either they will get off or you will get off. That is just the way it is.

You decide what highway you ride on. You decide how many miles is your journey. At any point, you can let go of the programming, let go of the fear of the unknown, and simple BECOME. When you BECOME, you are free. And, in the moment of freedom all things are known and all life become perfect.

At any moment of your life you have the opportunity to evolve.

Human Nature

As human beings we each have a very specific set of emotions and desires. These emotions and desires spread out across the entire human race. We each hope to be happy, (not sad), safe, secure, protected, well-fed, (not hungry), intellectually and artistically stimulated, fulfilled, and supported by people we love and who love us. Though there are many more attributes that could be added to this list, these are the basic ones that can be used to define us as human beings. In association with these generalized parameters, each individual lives a life that is acutely focused upon one of more of these factors.

When one enters the spiritual path they are continually told that if one is to be truly spiritual they must leave behind all of the trapping of the human mind and body and enter into a space above and beyond all of the factors that define human existence. It must be understood, however, that each religion and each philosophic school of thought has their own set of parameters about which of the above defined human conditions are acceptable and which ones must be shunned. The problem with this whole negating philosophy is, however, that it sets one apart from the natural progression of human life and removes one from what actually defines us a human beings.

The response that is made by many religious pundits when presented with this fact is, *"But this is what the spiritual path is all about. The truly spiritual person is not defined by the constraints of human definition and, therefore, need not be bound by these or any other human factors."*

But, it must be understood that if that were the case, these primary human emotions and desires would not be the defining factors of the entire species. Therefore, for all of the various schools of religious thought to teach the practice of renunciation is, in fact, against the essence of humanity. Furthermore, if what these ascetic sects taught were elementally valid, than they would all be teaching the same philosophy. But, this not the case. They each have a different set of teachings with a different set of foundational logic for what they teach their members to overcome and leave behind. In fact, throughout the history of humanity, there has been no one emotion or desire that has been universally rejected. Each society and each culture, throughout time, has laid down their own set of definitions for appropriate human and spiritual behavior. Even at this specific juncture of time, how many churches, religious sects, and philosophies propagate vastly different philosophies?

This being stated, virtually anyone who walks the spiritual path is programmed to hold onto the belief that to be more, better, or more holy, that they must reject all things human and leave behind all emotion and desire. From this, every time a person on the spiritual path has a desire for love, for sex, for a better life, or whatever, they instantly believe that they are somehow less holy than their teacher, their guru, or some saint who lived a thousand years ago. But, at the true heart of spirituality this is all nonsense.

Fierce Grace

One of the great things about this modern age of the internet is that you can watch movies on your computer. Recently I was watching the film they made about Ram Dass soon after he had suffered his stroke. At the beginning of the movie he discusses, when he was experiencing the stroke, they took him to the hospitable and he felt nothing spiritual. He stated in essence, *"There I was, Mr. Spiritual and there was nothing. It made me realize I still had some work to do."*

My first thought to this scene and statement sent me back to my teenage years, when one of close spiritual friends and I actually sat around discussing and questioned the true spirituality of Ram Dass. This was when he and western spiritual was at its height in the mid 1970s. As Rolling Stone magazine put it, he was, *"Riding the Holyman Circuit."* For a moment, my mind said, *"I thought so…"*

As the documentary progress, Ram Dass is talking to an audience from his wheelchair and he is running pray beads through his fingers. My mind thought, *"What a poser…"*

The movie progresses further and it goes to archival footage when Ram Dass had first returned from India and was hosting a large numbers of people at his father's estate. It was almost as if I had forgotten how beautiful this period of time was. When spirituality was blooming. Everybody had long hair, didn't shave, and was truly attempting to embrace the spiritual essence of life. It was a truly glorious period of time. Love was in the air and the possibilities were endless.

There at the center of this scene was Ram Dass, walking around with his all-knowing persona -- having taken acid for years and having return from India with a new knowledge. He was the center of it. He was the center of the birth of the teachings. He was the vehicle.

Yes, the affluence he had grown up within allowed him to walk the life path he had chartered. But, this was simply his karma and he made the most of what he was given. Think about how many other people have grown up with affluence and have done nothing with their lives but fulfill their own momentary desires. This was and is not the case with Ram Dass.

Spirituality

Spirituality always came easy for me. I guess that was just my karma. We each have our own karma or destiny and it is our choice what we do with it. I was always able to instantly embrace the spiritual and to see the spiritual in what appeared to be just the opposite. And, from the moment I heard the Zen Buddhist philosophy that we are ALL already enlightened, we just have to realize it, I immediately comprehended this ideology. So, when someone questions their own spirituality, their own enlightenment, or holds onto the belief that they have more spiritual work to do, it sets a different set of thoughts off in my mind, than may be experiences by another person who simply accepts what the individual who is speaking has to say.

In any case, for Ram Dass to question his spirituality is simply mind-stuff. And, we each have our own set of mind-stuff. That is simply his. Why does he need more work? Look at what he unleashed. He helped to usher in a mindset that positively changed the world forever. And though, in many ways, the patterns of the world have shifted away from the essence he brought from India, that is just the nature of life and society. But, it does not diminish what he achieved.

Humanity is a desire driven species. For some of us, our desire was and is to spread the essence of spirituality. And, for a time in our recent history, it was embraced. But then, the masses were guided down another road. And, this is just the way it is. Life changes, society changes… But, for those of us who lived through that period of time, the essence will never be forgotten.

Perhaps in some time in the future, the essential elements of universal spiritually will again be remembered and embraced -- a space where whatever religion you are is fine, all that mattered is that we walk together, holding hands, and embracing each other's uniqueness. Hopefully…

The Teacher

Though great sages like J. Krishmurti choose to renounce their path as a formal guru. They none-the-less lived the path of a teacher. This too is the case of Ram Dass.

When you live the path of a teacher, your teachings are out there. What you say becomes public record. And, with this, the masses, (including myself), are allowed to judge, question, and reflect upon your words. Why? Because this is the essence of human nature and it is the curse of the teacher. This is human existence.

Which brings me back to the primary point of this writing. We are Human! No matter how hard we try to fight this fact. No matter how hard we try to transcend the limitations of this factor. No matter how many times we are told that we can ascent to some abstract realm of universal enlightenment and sainthood, we are still human. We are constrained by the factors of human nature. For this reason, we must stop trying to alienate our true nature. We must be who we are -- Human.

This is not to say that we should not strive to be more -- to be the best that we can be and to help humanity, by and means possible, within the constrains of our society, our culture, and our specific point in history.

What this does mean is that we must reject all of the people who pretend to be all-knowing. Who tell us all of the things we should not do and the things we must do to cause our consciousness to ascend. Why? Because throughout history it has been proven time and time again that the people who claim this all-knowingness have universally be found to be the ones who are simply basing their perceptions upon borrowed knowledge and ego-gratification. And, inevitably they are proven to be the ones who have fallen prey to all things they have condemned.

As I always say, *"Let go and be Free. Trust yourself. Hurt no one. Do good things. From this, your life and all of humanity will fall into perfection."*

Are You Forgiven?

The concept of forgiveness is essential element of spiritual evolution that must be brought into a very clear perspective for those of us who walk upon the spiritual path. This is predicated upon the fact that it is taught in all spiritual traditions that each of us has the potential for sin or, in other words, we each have the potential to do bad things. From a very fundamentalist position, based in the ancient Judaic Christian traditions, we are told that we all sin each time we have thoughts of lust, greed, embrace laziness, and so on. From the eastern perspective, it is a taught that desire is one of the primary acts that makes us unholy. From these fundamental traditions, people have felt unworthy and have mentally and physically punished themselves throughout the centuries.

When one looks at the remedies for these abstract sins, perhaps the most appealing is that provided by the Catholic Church. Here, when one has sinned they go to a priest, confess their sins, and are given absolution once they have performed the assigned amount of recited Catholic mantras: i.e. *"Our Father's,"* or *"Hail*

Mary's." Similarly, in the Protestant Religion, a practitioner is told that they are absolved from past sins once they are baptized or rebaptized into the Christian faith.

Though these physical actions may well make an individual who follows a particular religious tradition feel better about them self, once they have indulged in an action they believe to be a sin, there is a problem with these traditions of sin absolution, however. This takes place when an individual goes to a priest or minister to be absolved from a more concrete sin -- when they have physically, mentally, or emotionally wronged or hurt another person.

The fact is, though a priest or minister may absolve a person of what they have done, I doubt that the individual who was hurt would be as willing to simply accept the priest's absolution of the sinning individual. Therefore, is the sin forgiven? No, it is not. A priest or minister does not possess the power to forgive a sin that was unleashed upon another human being.

Therefore, as we each have encountered situation where we have been injured by others, (by an untold number of methods), we must study the inflicting of damage or pain onto other people in order to come to a clearer perspective of the root cause for the infliction of pain and, thereby, come to understand the pathway to forgiveness. From this, we each can learn to remain conscious and unbound by the actions of others and the world as we walk though our Life Time.

The Idea of Forgiveness
The idea of forgiveness is an interesting concept for those of us who care about such things. I say this because there are many people who walk the face of the earth who do not care what they do or who they injure in their quest to gain what they desire, be in money, power, sex, fame, possessions, control over other people, etc. This is perhaps the primary understanding one must embrace when they begin to ponder forgiveness. The fact is, some people feel guilt and some do not. If you feel guilt for things that you have done, when you have harmed other, than you care about forgiveness -- if you do not, then the thought of forgiveness does not enter your mind. The problem with this rejective mindset is, however, if you embrace it, you will be shunned from higher awareness and kept from living a truly fulfilled life as long as you maintain this low level of consciousness.

For those individuals who do not care what they do or whom they injure in the conquest of what they hope to gain are those people who live a very hollow existence. Though they may gain what they want in a particular moment of time, they are also the one's who pay for their acquisition in the long run of their life.

The actions of these unconscious people span the gambit from stealing or shoplifting things for no good reason: i.e. not for the need to keep their body or the bodies of their family alive. Damaging other people's property for sport. And, inflicting emotional pain on a person by not taking that individual's emotions into consideration while selfishly performing acts which are self-motivated.

Certainly, we can each think of a million subdivisions of these broad categories -- things that have occurred to us or to others that we know. But, at the root of all of these actions is the acting individual's inconsideration for what effect they are having on another person or person(s) life.

You see, the reality of life is, what you do affects other people. If you do something negative, what you are doing will effect another person, negatively. Now, you may pretend to believe that what you are doing will have no effect, or what you are doing is not actually inflicting damage, but this is a completely inaccurate mindset. In fact, you may believe that due to the fact that you blame your parents, your family, your friends, someone who hurt you in the past, or society on the whole for casting you into an existence that you wished would be different, that you have the right to do anything that you what to do to whomever you want to do it to. Or, from a secondary perspective, you may falsely believe that you have the right to take some abstract revenge on another person for some nondescript action you feel they perpetrated upon you. In any case, the fact of the matter is, if you are doing negative things that only breeds more negativity. If you embrace negativity, if you act out on negatively, then negativity will continually follow you, and it is you who will pay the ultimate price if you do not take the conscious action to remedy what you have broken or damaged. You are the center of the universe. Good or bad emanates from you.

The Two States of Consciousness

There are two primary states of consciousness in this world: those who care about others and those who care about themselves. Which are you?

People who truly care about other people and are always trying to make the world a better place are obvious. Their actions speak for themselves and they move forward through life continually encountering positive situations where personal growth and positive life-force is present. On the other hand, people who only care about themselves and live a life dominated by damaging others, other's property, and fulfilling their own momentary desires are those who are left always wanting, and questioning why life has passed them by, what did they do wrong, why do they not possess what they truly had hoped for, and so on. These are the people who are continually burdened by abstract dilemmas that continue to haunt their life. Why? Because they have chosen to chart their existence on a path where they do bad things. Even if they try to help someone, they do this from a position of desire -- of wanting to do the action in order to obtain a desired result. So, their giving becomes meaningless.

In many cases, these individuals, at a deeper level, know that they have lived a life where they have done bad things and are performing these actions as an abstract means to clean their karma. But, these actions never work, because they are not remedying what they have actually broken with the person or persons they actually caused harm to or damaged, they are simply following the path of unthinking selfishness they have previously embraced and trying to buy back their purity.

This is not to say that any individual, at any point in their life, cannot change their life course. What they need to do is as the Catholic practitioner goes to their priest to confess their sins, they must acknowledge and confess their wrong activities, then they must follow a path where they consciously remedy the damage they have committed.

Forgiveness

You commonly hear, when a person or family has been wronged, that they make the statement, *"I forgive the person."* But, what does that mean? If someone has done something bad to you, it will be remembered. Forgiving them means nothing.

Many people claim, from a psychological perspective, if you have been wronged that you must forgive a person to be whole and complete again if you wish to move forward with your life. But, who and what are you forgiving when a person does not acknowledge their negative actions and attempt to remedy their wrongs? What are

55

you accomplishing by forgiving if an individual deserves no forgiveness? The fact of the matter is most people who live a life embracing negativity never truly seek forgiveness. They only claim that they do once they are captured by law enforcement or are put on the spot in front of family or friends, and so on. Therefore, they are not truly seeking forgiveness. They are simply stating words in order to calm the emotions of those around them. In other words, they are lying.

Someone who seeks forgives sets about on a path to consciously fix what they have broken and repair the lives of those they have damaged. The reality is, and I have stated this for decades, it is very easy to break something, it is much harder to repair it. But, the person who truly seeks forgiveness must walk down that road and do whatever it takes to fix what they have broken. And no, going to a priest, confessing your sins, being baptized or rebaptized, or reciting a mantra will not cleanse you.

What should those who have been wronged do to move forward with their lives, if symbolic forgiveness is not the answer? They must just move forward and live. Embrace the positive and all negativity will be destroyed. As it has been proven so many times in life -- oftentimes what occurs to a person who has been wrong is that they grow from the experience and, in fact, their life moves to a better place. This is one of the cosmic laws of the universe.

If you are on the other end of the spectrum and have damaged the lives of others, either in small or large ways, what should you do? Fix what you have broken!

Ultimately, we, as evolving human beings, must care about one another. We should do all that we can to make the lives of other people better, not worse. And, this does not mean that you should give a person what you think they need. It means, make their lives better by their own definition of the word.

By making the lives of other people better, then the entire world becomes a more whole and accepting place. With this as a basis for human interaction, people gain respect and love for one other. If, on the other hand, people are hurt, injured, or disrespected, then that mindset is also breed in the individual and it, therefore, spreads out across the planet. So, choose to be positive. Choose to do the right thing. Stop think solely about your own momentary desires and make this world a better place because this LIFE is that we know, it is all that we have.

The Silence of Mind

On virtually every spiritual paths, the concept of meditation is taught to its practitioners. Though the techniques for meditation vary from teaching to teaching, the desired results are the same -- a calm, one-pointedness of mind and, at advanced levels, interaction with the divine.

Though virtually all spiritual paths discuss meditation, there are many people who question its usefulness in modern society. Though the concept of a calm, one-pointed mind, and divine interaction all sound very good, for an untold number of reasons people choose not to meditate.

One of the primary reasons people forgo meditation is the time it takes to actually bring the body and mind into a place where meditation may be actualized. With society so full of places to be and things to do, many people feel they just do not have the time. It was for this reason that spiritual schools of thought such as Transcendental Meditation were developed. In TM it is taught that success in meditation can be had simply by sitting down for a few minutes a day.

Other schools of meditation developed that embraced a concentration on playing a musical instrument, on dancing, on walking, bowing, shooting a bow and arrow, painting, making flower arrangements, serving tea, and so on. In each of these cases, these schools of meditation were developed for those people who did not possess the mindset to believe that they possessed the time or the metal focus to actually sit down and meditate.

Anyone who plays a musical instrument will quickly attest to the fact that is a very focused action. Formal dancer will say the same thing. As will painters, martial artists, and tea ceremony masters. But, the results differ greatly between meditating by focusing on an external object or physical action and consciously sitting down and silencing the mind.

Why Sit?

Life is a complicated place. Events happen to all of us that cause us to lose our peace and remove our focus on what we truly hope to actualize and achieve. Some people are lucky, they work in an environment where their coworkers all get along and they live in a safe neighborhood. Others are born into or develop the financial means to remove many of the obstacles of life. Though this is the case for some, most of us are left to a world where we have to interact with people who are not focused on consciousness and are set on a path of solely getting what they want by whatever means possible. From this, each of us has, at least, visited a Life-Place where conflict occurred.

It is the simple reality of life that we each must find a way to move from birth to death, while trying to remain healthy, happy, and whole which encountering instances that we wish would never have happened. This is just the condition of life. For better or for worse, this is the way it is. Who ever said life was fair?

When these life situations occur, it is very common for the average person to completely freak out. Why, because they are overcome with emotion. And, emotion equals enhanced adrenal flow. For some they become addicted to this rush of adrenaline. These are the kind of people who tell you that they love their job -- that their job is their meditation, even though it is obviously a very stressful environment and you can see that it is damaging their health. But, for most, when life goes wrong, or a stressful even is encountered, living itself becomes very hard and the question of, *"Why,"* or *"Why me,"* echoes in the mind.

First of all, there is no answer to this. Life is life and things are going to happen. We can each consciously place ourselves in an environment where we will meet as few obstacles as possible, but sooner or later things will happen that we do not like.

What this has to do with meditation is that, when these evens occur, as stated, the average person freaks out. They are driven to acting out all kinds of events like anger, sadness, high blood pressure, anxiety, and even suicide. But, on the other hand, for someone who consciously meditates, they have developed the ability to focus their mind and guide it to a place of peace, where answers to the problem can be understood and living through the event will be less emotionally devastating.

What do you do when you sit and meditate? Just like when you lift weights or run, you are developing a muscle. In the case of meditation, it is the muscle that acutely focuses your mind.

When you sit and meditate, you are focusing on a very singular object -- be it a mantra, your breath, an image of what you perceive the divine entity to be, and so on. What you achieve by doing this is the ability to remove your mind from the chaos of the world, and take it to a place where divine understanding and perpetual peace may be encountered. It if for this reason that choosing to sit and meditate can actually provide you with the tools you need to emotionally overcome even the most trying of circumstances.

So, the next time you tell yourself that you do not have the time to practice meditation or you do not possess the mental mindset to sit and focus your mind for a few minutes a day, think about what the not taking the time to perform these action will mean to you the next time a situation of intensity or stress comes your way. Believe me, it is far better to be mentally prepared and exercise the muscle of your mind when you have some down time than when you get hit over the head with an excessive life event.

SIT!

Planned Parenthood

I was driving home from having lunch in San Pedro; listen to, *Jonesy's Jukebox,* on the radio. Steve Jones, probably most noted for being the guitar player in the Sex Pistols, hosts this radio show.

Normally, when he has guests, they are musicians. But, this day there were two girls who were talking about New Age philosophy.

They proceeded to discuss reincarnation. They stated the reason we keep reincarnating is that each time we are sent to a new physical body is because of the fact that we want to learn a very specific thing about life. They continued, of course, we don't realize this until we die and then, once we have left our physical body, we can analyze whether or not we actually learned the knowledge that we had hoped to acquire. They also stated that what takes place before we enter our current body is that we each, (somewhere up there, in some ethereal heaven), actually choose the parents that we are born to in order to actualize our path of specific knowledge acquisition.

I listened for a few moments and then changed station. I was just dumfounded by the borrowed knowledge that they were spewing -- words that had been regurgitated by so many others before them. I mean, since the moment I entered the spiritual path, all those years ago, I have heard versions of that same nonsensical discourse spoken by those who want to appear spiritual - hoping to sound as if they know some deep-dark secret about the origin and evolution of life. What nonsense.

This is the problem with the novice on the spiritual path -- they believe everything that they hear and then they want to repeat it. Most, however, never leave this novice level of spiritual consciousness and, thus, never rise to a state of true wisdom. This is why they simply continue to repeat what they heard -- be it true or false.

But, let's take a minute here and think about what those two ladies were saying. They claim that we each choose our own parents before we are born. If this is the case, it means that our parents have no choice in the matter. They are simply infested with a soul that has chosen them. If this were true, that would mean that only the ethereal-bound entities have the right of choice and the living are simply the receptacles of the desires of the ethereal being that want to use them as the vehicle to learn what they desire to learn. If you were to believe this explanation it would detail that the ethereal beings are simply desire bound entities that are seeking something -- good or bad and are using the bodies, in association with the physical, psychological, and the sociological makeup, of the earth bound parents to provide them a pathway to fulfilling their desired ends.

This is the problem with humanity as a whole. Instead of seeking the truth from within, humans concoct ridiculous abstract rational for the meaning of life. Then, the design elaborate philosophic rational to explain why these developed ideologies are happening. And, this previously described discourse is just one example. Each religion and philosophy, throughout time, has designed its own set of ridiculous tenets that it then claims to be the truth and orchestrates intricate stories so that they can claim it has factual possibilities.

Seriously, if one existed in the ethereal, heavenly realm, why would they need to return to earth and this physical existence to learn anything? Aren't the ethereal, heavenly realms the source point for all knowledge? I mean, come on, if you are in the ethereal realm and have the ability to do things like choose your parents, which means you have dominion over humans, why would you need to learn anything from the human race?

But, this is the human condition; we want to explain the abstract realms of, *"Why."* But, *"Why,"* will never be explained.

From the dawn of human consciousness to the end of it, there were and will be those who claim to know. But, if what they knew was the absolute truth, there would be no question and no other, *"Knower,"* would ever be claiming a different set of religious possibilities or stating that what another person believes is false.

Knowledge is a personal perspective. What you know is what you know. But, be careful; don't confuse what you believe with what you know, because they are two completely different things.

Ultimately, we all just are. If you can accept that it is not important to know all of the answers of the universe, then you are free. If you are free then you don't have to recite someone else's brand of borrowed knowledge. From this, the nonsense of humanity is laid to rest and all of humanity becomes free.

Zen is Free.

Getting What You Want

To begin this discussion we all can agree that everybody wants something. Some people want money, some want fame, and some want power. While others want inner peace, world peace, or to help the less fortunate overcome their limitations.

Even a being whose teaching became as universally embraced as Siddhartha Guatama, the Buddha, wanted something. He wanted enlightenment. This desire set him on his path to obtaining it. And, from his realizations, he made one of the most profound statements ever recorded throughout human history, *"The cause of suffering is desire."*

Though the Buddha made this statement, and most of us universally agree with its truth, none-the-less, mankind or womankind continues to seek out the gaining of Some-Thing.

What Do You Want

What do You Want? And, why do you want it? This is the question that must be asked by anyone who walks the path of consciously obtaining his or her desire. But, here lies one of the primary problems with what people want and why they don't get it. They don't get it because, *"They,"* do not clearly know why they want it.

It is easy to say, *"I want more money." "I want to save the world." "I want to be famous." "I want love." "I want sex." "I want whatever..."* But, why do you want it? And, if you get it, what will obtaining it mean?

Now, for some desires it is very clear why you want them. For example, you live in bad conditions and you want to move away from them. Okay, that's understandable. What are you going to do about it?

Which brings up the next complexity on the path to obtaining what you want -- action.

We all want something. But, what are you going to do to obtain your desire? And, can that desire even be obtained?

Restrictions and Attributes

The moment we are born, we are all supplied with a set of restriction. These restrictions are based in our physical, psychological, cultural, and socioeconomic makeup. For example, a person born into poverty in India may have the desire to become a Wall Street Powerbroker, but the reality of them obtaining that end goal is fairly impossible.

This is one of the key problems with the desire-full mindset of a person born in the western world. We hear story-upon-story of someone who rose from the depth of society and became highly successful. The common belief is, *"If they can do it, why can't I?"*

Well, there is a lot of reasons why you can't do it.

The majority of life is based upon luck and the draw of the cards. We are each defined by our life restrictions. Hand-in-hand with these restrictions we are each defined by our life attributes.

Just as we each are provided a set of restrictions, we are also given as set of attributes. Your attributes are defined by the same parameters as your restrictions and more. Here, particularly, personality comes into play.

Many people falsely believe that a person creates their own personality. Though we can guide our own personality to a certain degree, the reality is, we are born with a personality. It is then shaped further by the influences in our early years.

Yes, we each develop our own set of desires. In some cases, these desires may be far from those embraced by our peer group.

But, none-the-less, we make these choices defined by the personality we are provided with at birth. For better or worse, that is the truth.

Desire

All this being stated, we each still want what we want. We each have our own desire(s).

To put these desires into a proper context, to see if we can actually get what we want, we must initially come to a clear understanding of the possibilities of achieving said desires are, or we will be cast to a life lived unfulfilled, frustrated, and angry.

Think about it, how many people do you know that have set their goals so high that they can never be achieved and these unfulfilled desires have left them very unhappy at their not being obtained? So, before you set out on a path of desire obtainment, you must clearly define what your desire is and then take a long hard look at yourself and decide whether or not there is an actual chance of you obtaining it.

If there is, go for it. If not, don't. It's as simple as that.

Visualization

Since the beginning of the, *"New Age,"* there have been scores of teachers who have taught the practice of *Visualization*. In brief, what *Visualization* promises is that if you focus very hard on what you want, you will get. Well maybe...

But, what is more important to initially look at is the teachers who teach this practice.

As stated we all want something. And, we all want a promise of a way to achieve it. In *Visualization,* it is promised, all you have to do is see it clearly in you mind's eye and you will achieve it.

Think about it. How many people have written books about *Visualization?* And, though the techniques in these books vary slightly, they all teach the same thing.

It is similar with *Feng Shui*. People write books on the subject. They provide all kinds of examples of how this person's life totally changed once they rearranged their home or their business. But, this is just talk. There is no proof of it. And, if the fortunes of person's life did change, was it based on *Feng Shui* or just an evolving of their destiny?

Again, think about it. How many lectures and seminars have been given on the subjects of *Visualization* and *Feng Shui?* Do these authors and lecturers do this for free? No, they do not. They get paid. Some of them get paid a lot of money. So, in reality, you are helping them fulfill their desires of fame and fortune while you buy into the same promise that has been spoken about for generations.

The reality of *Visualization* is that, yes, if you focus on something it will be clearly defined in your mind. But, if you do not take the physical actions to obtain your goal, it can never be achieved. It is not simply going to magically appear.

Gifts From God

Many people, when they get some object that they truly desire, attribute it to a gift from god. And, maybe it is…

But, the reality of life is, you only appreciate obtaining something if it was what you were looking for. For example, say you want a physical item such as a specific watch. All of a sudden you find that watch very cheap in a store. You are so excited, *"Thank you god!"* But, think about how many people passed by that very same watch and didn't even notice it. They didn't desire it, so even if they saw it, it would have had no effect on them. But, you desired it, so it is a great gift.

Now, this is the reality of obtaining desires and it is the root source of visualization. You have to want it. So, what do you want?

If you want a specific object, you can probably obtain it. You think about it. You define exactly what you want. You look for it. You save your money. And, you buy it. It is yours. Desire fulfilled.

If you want a person, this is where the whole process becomes sketchy. Why? Because each person has their own set of desires. And, desires change constantly. So, just because you want a person, does not mean that they will want you. Or, just because a person wanted you at one stage of their life, does not mean that they will want you forever.

The moment you bring personality into the equitation, the process of visualization becomes convoluted. Because no matter how much you want a person, if they don't want you, they don't want you.

This is also the problem when people set their eyes on becoming a major movie star, a rock star, or a revered author. Sure, people have done it before. But, just because they have done it, does not mean that you have the luck or karma to do the same thing. Success in those industries is rarely based upon talent. Success is based primarily upon luck. Plus, so many individuals define the road to success in those industries. And, these individuals are defined by so much ego and desires of their own that to simply attempt to visualize your way through them is impossible.

Which bring is to defining your desires…

Defining Your Desires

Spiritual teachers will tell you, *"Have no desires."* But, let's face reality, everybody, even the spiritual teacher, has desires. So, what are you going to do to achieve your desire?

If it's a physical desire: a car, a house, travel to a foreign country, it is pretty easy. Stop screwing around, get a job, save your money, and obtain it.

If your desire is another person, be ready to let go of that desire if they do not want you. Do not mess up their life and your life by being a hanger-on. If they want you, they want you. If they don't, they don't. And, nothing is going to change that. Stop lying to yourself that they will come around. Move on to a new desire. Put yourself out there, go to places, go to events, and meet someone who actually appreciates who you are.

If your desire is a grandiose goal: to be a movie star, an award winning filmmaker, a rock star, a novelist, a captain of industry, or whatever, set about on a course to obtaining it. But, do it with the understanding that you will not let that desire dominant your entire existence; because living life in that fashion will destroy you.

Do what you do to achieve your desire. Take classes, get a video camera and make small films, play music, write words. And, most importantly, let people know that you are doing it. The best way to do that is the Internet. As we all understand, the Internet has changed the world.

In other words, DO! Because doing is the ultimate visualization.

Do not sit around hoping, dreaming, believing, focusing, and fantasizing that just because you want something it will happen. It will not. You must DO.

Finally, we all have desires. We can allow our desires to control our entire existence. But, that is a very selfish state of mind. We can allow the not obtaining of them to destroy us. But, that is not the path of consciousness.

But, what we can consciously do is realize that we all want. We all have desires. We can also understand that just because we want, that does not mean that we will get. We can try. But, at the end of the day we each have to realize the truth in the words of the Buddha, *"The cause of suffering is desire."*

Desire, because that is a condition of life. Desire, but do not be controlled by your desire. Do not allow them to guide you down a path of evil, larceny, or destruction. Because then, all you will ever be defined by is the negative you unleashed.

Desire, but be positive in the obtainment of your desire.

In the process of obtaining it, find a way to give back, to provide, and to positively change the lives of those you encounter as you seek its obtainment. Because then, even if you don't obtain a specific desire, you will have made a contribution, as small as it may be, to the lives of those you encountered and the overall betterment of the world.

A Position of Authority

I think that it is always interesting watching the fervor in which people attack individuals in positions of authority -- particularly religious authority. This seems to be a byproduct of this modern, very litigious, society that we live in. The primarily cause of this is greed.

Let's face it, an attack on any person; in a position of authority, it is based upon two things. First of all, the person who is on the attack wishes to dethrone the individual they are attacking. They want to make them appear to be less, in the eyes of others.

Why do they want to do this? Because they do not believe the individual is worthy -- for whatever reason. What their ideology is based upon, however, is ego and insecurity. Why? Because a person who has achieved something in life has no need to behave in this fashion. They have accomplished what they have accomplished, are secure in that accomplishment, and, therefore, base their life from a perspective of self-worth. Thus, they have no reason to go after another person of accomplishment because they are secure in themselves.

As I always say, *"You do not have the right to criticize anyone until you have, at least, achieved what he or she has achieved."*

The second reason that an individual in a position of authority is attacked is because the person attacking wants money. They believe by going after this individual they will somehow remove the wealth they have achieved and put it in their own pockets. They do this, primarily, by suing.

I think that we have all heard stories about people being sued for whatever reason -- you particularly hear about these situations when a person has some level of fame or notoriety. Maybe you have been sued?

I too have encountered this style of nonsensical situation. For example, this occurred to me when this one individual, who was lying about his martial arts credentials and was attempting to diminish mine, (an occurrence which, unfortunately, has become very prominent in the modern martial arts). In any case, he threatened to sue me for stating that he was a liar. I said, *"Go ahead."* This guy was eventually discredited but, as we have discussed, he tried to make himself more by basing his reality upon lies and attacking me.

Another situation happen to me when a lady hit me with her car, when I was riding my motorcycle, and almost killed me. Then, she sued me. Of course, she didn't win. But, I mean how ridiculous was that?

Another, even more amusing situation happened to me when a guy came up to me and was attempting to start a fight. Now, I am one of those people who avoids confrontations whenever possible, because they are generally so meaningless. But, just before it got physical, he said, *"You're probably going to beat me up and after you do, I'm going to call the police, have you arrested, and then I'm going to sue you."* At least he was honest. But, this society has gotten so ridiculous that you can't even go *mano-a-mano* anymore without the threat of a lawsuit.

People somehow assume that if they threaten to sue you, you will kowtow and give into their wishes. Whenever I have encountered these situations, I tell these people, *"Go ahead,"* because at the end of the day, the only people who get rich from lawsuits are the lawyers. And, I just won't play that game. And besides, they would be pretty disappointed in the size of my bank account if they ever saw it anyway.

But, the point I am making is that this goes back to the whole concept of greed, at whatever level. A person who has not achieved anything of importance in their own life, and wishes that they had, wants what another person, in a position of authority, possesses. This is based upon any number of psychological insecurities and the lack of personal achievement.

The ultimate question is, *"What does a person in a position of authority have that other's do not? And, why have they achieved what they have achieved, when other's have not?"*

To answer, what they have is the one-pointed drive and focus to achieve. And, this is the primary reason why they have achieved what they have achieved. On the other side of the coin, the lack of this drive and one-pointed focus is what has caused others to not achieve and to fail.

I am not saying that everything that a person in a position of authority does is right -- far from it. What I am saying is that what caused them to rise up to their level of socioeconomic evolution is, *"Drive,"* combined with a little bit of luck.

Drive is not something you can give a person. Some are born with it. Other's, simply focus their attention to the degree that they achieve what they want to achieve in life. But, once they have achieved their initial desired level of success, then they are confronted by those who want to see them fall from grace.

If you ever find yourself in the position of envy or wishing the demise of another individual, you have to ask yourself, *"What does that person have that I do not? And, why have the achieved it, when I have not?"* This is not a complicated question and the answer, if you are true to yourself, should come very easily.

There are positive people in this world and there are negative people. It is as simple as that -- yin and yang. Some people base their lives on helping others, while others sit around complaining and attacking others when they have no basis to do so. So, again, I get back to one of the primary points, *"If you have not achieved what the person you are attacking has achieved, you have no right to attach them, because you are not living your life on the same level of existence as they are."*

Damages

Many people have been programed by this modern society to believe that when they feel damaged by a person, in a position of authority, they are, thereby, owed money. But, what does money have to do with damages. I mean if you get in a wreck, the insurance company of the person who hit your car should pay for it to be fixed. But, once a car has been wrecked, it is never the same. And, this is the perfect example about life. Once something is broken, it can never truly be fixed. It can be bandaged and repaired. The scars can be covered up. But, the life is never the same.

This is simply the reality of this place we call LIFE. From each encounter, we emerge a changed and different person. Sometime this is a good experience; sometimes it is not. But, the reality of it is, we are changed. What we do with the change is up to us.

Many people, who are on the leaving-side of a relationship, are very bitter. What they wanted, a happy life, forever-and-ever, did not happen. So, they are very angry with their partner and they want to get even. This is particularly the case if the person they were in a relationship was a person in a position authority. They want revenge.

I was just reading about Swami Kriyananda and how he got sued by a couple of his devotees who he apparently had sex with. Now, back-in-the-day, if you wanted to have sex with somebody, you did. And, that was that. You didn't sue them if they didn't answer every need and desire you ever imagined.

I mean, Get real people! You are adults! You can make choices! Just like everyone one else can make choices. If you make the choice to have sex, you made that choice. Nobody forced you into it. It was just a choice you made. If you feel guilty, bad, or whatever afterwards, that is your fault. Live with it! If you are in a relationship, at whatever level, and the other person chooses to leave, that is their choice. People have the right to make choices.

We all make our own choice in life. Some are good, some are bad. Some we wish we hadn't made. But, it is you, individually, who made that choice. You cannot later blame a person and sue them because you are sorry about the choice you made. That is so empty, so irresponsible, and it means that you are not, *"Owning,"* anything that you have done. It is very unspiritual.

I have read so many times about this person suing that spiritual teacher, because they had sex. Now, I am not discussing the sick priests who mess with young children or the pseudo religious pundits who lead their flock into prostitution or mass suicide. But, in all other cases, you are an adult. You make your own choices.

If you later regret being with a person, you have to ask yourself, *"Why did I want to be that person in the first place?"* The answer will probably be that you were attracted to them because they were in a position of authority and it made you feel special that they wanted to be in a personal relationship with you.

Own your choices! And, quit trying to make other people pay when they choose to no longer be with you.

An extreme example of this happened in my realms of vision. It occurred when this very beautiful girl, who worked as a waitress, at a restaurant I used to frequent seemed to disappear. I mean people change jobs all the time. So, I didn't give it a lot of thought. In any case, I didn't see her for a time and then she returned and her face was mangled. And, when I say mangled, I mean mangled. Apparently, she had gotten involved with a seedy guy who was really into drugs and he flipped the jeep they were driving in, out in the desert. What happened to him, I do not know. But her... It was very sad.

She moved on with her life. As she was a waitress, she had no health insurance and a limited income, so she could not afford extensive plastic surgery. Yet, I would see her, waiting her tables, with a smile on her face. She always, at least, appeared to be happy.

I often wondered how anyone could do that -- go back to a place where everyone remembered her beauty and pretend nothing was wrong. Yet, she did it.

Eventually, she got married and had some kids and her life moved forward. If someone can overcome that, who are any of these people to claim that some individual caused them some sort of unbearable damage, simply because they no longer wanted to be them and moved forward onto a new relationship?

It is like all of the jilted wives (or husbands) of movie or sports stars that you hear about. In their divorce they expect to get all of this money, cars, houses, or whatever from their former spouse. But, why do they deserve it? What did they do that was great or notable? All they did was marry someone and the relationship eventually fell apart. Why should they get half or more or the person's estate? They accomplished nothing. Because, *"I put up with the person,"* is not a qualifier. That is simply what you do when you enter into a relationship -- put up with somebody; good or bad.

It is like the story one of my teachers, Swami Satchidananda, used to tell. He would say, Relationship are like doing business. As long as you say, *"I love you, honey."* They will respond with, *"Oh, I love you too."* But, the moment you say, *"I don't love you anymore."* They answer, *"Then, I hate you."* But, if love is love then you would love a person whether they loved you or not, no matter what. But, this is not the case; love is a business.

This is the same condition of life. People turn to a person in a position of authority because they like their teachings, their qualities, their success, their whatever. But, just like in love, when they are in their early stages of admiration, they are infatuated and blind to all the faults of this individual. And, believe me, we all have faults; we all have a personality, even the most so-called holy.

So, number one, if you want to seek out a person in a position of authority, understand that they are human, just like you. They possess hopes and desires, just like you. To achieve them, they may build upon their position of authority. If you are willing to give into their desires, that is fine. If not, you have the ability to say, *"No."* Don't blame them is you say, *"Yes."*

Secondarily, if you have some form of experience, with an individual in a position of authority, that you came away bruised and damaged from, you must realize that it was your own set of desires that led you into that situation. As such, there is no one to blame but you. Own that fact and quit trying to shift the blame away from your own desires, mindset, and hopes for the outcome of your life.

Finally, if you are on the side-lines and hope to move away from them, you will never be able to base any achievement on the meaningless attacking of a person in a position of authority. All this type of behavior does is to make you look envious, which is never attractive on any level. So, don't do it.

Whether are not you ever ascend to the level of those you either admire or hate is not important. What is important is that you live a life based in the realization of your own perfection. It is essential to note that attacking people will negate anything you may achieve.

Yes, you may love this person. Or, yes, may be a little bit jealous about what a particular individual has achieved and think you can do it better. Well, if you can, than do it. If not, then, be silent. Live you own perfection.

Do what you do, to the best of your ability and then all life moves to a much more conscious plane of existence and this world and this universe are left to embrace its own natural suchness.

This is Zen.

90

You Are Not A Christian

I was the only customer shopping in a small boutique. There were two employees in the shop having a heated discussion. I could not help but overhear their words. The one, a man, was stating that he believed that it was the fault of the immoral policies of the United States government that had unjustly imprisonment suspected terrorists at the prison at Guantanamo Bay and due to the harsh conditions they were forced to undergo, with no hope of a fair trail or release, that it was the fault of the United States government that some of these prisoners had committed suicide. The female employee argued that these people were simply mentally ill and, if they were not, they would have not committed suicide. The argument went back and forth with no end in sight until the man said, *"Well, if you believe that, that means that you're not a Christian."*

Throughout all levels of society this type of statement comes into play when a person is not getting their way in a conversation and/or argument. It is kind of like embracing the philosophy of, *"Well, since you won't agree with my point of view,*

I will simply kick you below the belt, to get my point across."

We have all witnessed discussions diminishing to this level of verbal assault. You may wonder, *"Why would someone add this style of dialogue to a discussion?"* To answer, it is added because from this style of rhetoric the topic completely changes.

After the employee in the boutique made his statement, the female employee exclaimed, *"What! I'm not a Christian! No, you're the one who isn't a Christian!"*

Ultimately this is the sad reality about opinions that equal discussions that ultimately lead to arguments -- people want to talk. They want to say what they believe. They want their point to be accepted. They want everyone else to embrace their philosophy. And, they want their opinion to be accepted as RIGHT by the masses. When it is not, then the rules of discourse go out the window and it becomes every man (or women) for themselves.

Why Participate?

The ultimate question you have to ask yourself is, *"Why should I participate in this style of discourse at all?"* Certainly, throughout life, we have all disagreed with what other people have said. For example, I was recently at a party in Orange County

California. For those of you who are not familiar with that region of the country, it is commonly understood to be a bastion of Caucasian Republican conservatism. I was sitting with a couple of friends at a table and a person came up, sat down, and blatantly began to state as fact that the reason gas prices were going up again was because it was a secret plan of President Obama. I said, *"No, it is because of world market demands and the speculation of investors."* Another person chimed in, stating that he was expecting Armageddon to occur any day now because Obama had been elected president and Obama was destroying the way the world views the United States. In disbelief I inquired, *"What do you think George W. Bush did?"*

The two ultra conservatives began to exchange agreeing banter. The three liberals, myself included, got up and left the conversation.

We Each Have Our Opinions

We each have our opinion. Some of our opinions are based on fact and some are based in belief. But, most people already have their minds made up about what they do and do not believe. It is for this reason that, for the most part, intellectual discussions among people of differing mindsets rarely prove anything. For example, try to discuss Christianity with a Christian -- detailing the true history of the religion to them, and you will run into a brick wall of denial of facts. First you will be told, *"It is all based in faith. And, faith is what our lord expects of us."* Then, if you still carrying on the discussion, you will ultimately be told, *"By the way, you know you are going to Hell for being a nonbeliever."*

This Life-Fact of differing opinions is the basis for all elements of conflict. So, first and foremost, before you even enter into one of these heated discussions, you have to decide, are you willing to entering into a conflict. If you are, you must first understand, that conflicts only end one way -- there is a winner and there is a loser. Now, the person of war may be willing to pay this price and live their life by this standard. But, this is emphatically NOT the spiritual way. The spiritual way is a path of peace and positivity - though many so-called spiritual people forget this fact when attempting to defend their ideology.

But the debative conflict of life is much more subtle than this. At the heart of all debate is the ideology of one person who has instigated the verbal confrontation. From that one person, the debate grows and grows and grows. But, no matter how big it gets, it is based upon the ideology of one person. And, what that person is propagating is most commonly based on attacking the thoughts, actions, and beliefs of another person or person(s).

Schadenfreude

It is somewhat like the German term, *"Schadenfreude,"* which can be translated in several ways but basically it refers to the fact that a person or persons takes joy in another person's demise or fall from grace. People who embrace this mindset look down upon the accomplishments of another and, in fact, find accomplishment a reason and motivation to denigrate and criticize people.

For whatever reason, people love to congregate in their own negativity. They love to band together and find a place where their voice of negativity can be heard and embraced. Some may say that this is a human condition. But, I don't believe that to be the case. The only reason that a person or person(s) may relish the demise of another is based in the fact that a negatively based person has not achieved the level of accomplishment or success they have desired in their chosen field. Or, if they have achieved a certain level of success, they feel that by bringing another person down they have become superior. But, higher and lower is all foolishness. Less or more is all a state of mind. And, less or more, higher or lower, is never a concept embraced by the truly spiritual individual.

From a personal perspective I have seen this many times. Someone will contact me being very friendly -- most commonly based upon the fact that they want something from me. Then, sometime later, I will find that this same person is speaking or writing very hash things about me, most commonly based upon lies and falsehoods.

Why do people choose to behave in this fashion? Because that is the mindset they have ultimately chosen to embrace. They have entered a space of negativity. And, this goes on throughout the world constantly. Think about it, how many people have you heard speaking negatively about someone they do not even know and have never met? The problem with this mindset and reaction based mentality is that all it produces is a nonsensical waste of LIFE TIME and LIFE ENERGY.

The question to ask yourself, if you find yourself embracing a negative mentality is, *"Do you feel good when you criticize others? Does it make you a better person? Does it make the world a better place?"* The answer will almost universally be, *"No."*

What behaving in this manner actually equals is that you are not contributing to the Greater-Good of this place we call Life. Instead, if you are following this negative level of human consciousness, you are not contributing to the betterment; you are only trying to destroy. And, destruction on any level is a negative pathway.

Think about the people you have admired. Do they follow a path of negativity or do they provide the world with a positive service? Think about the people who have made major contribution to the world. Are they negative and critical? Are they constantly involving themselves in criticism, arguments, and negative debates? No, they are not. No matter what field they are in, what they do is to do what they do. They continue to learn and grow as an individual, and follow a path that leads to the betterment of themselves and the world. They turn away from confrontations, verbal or otherwise. This is the path to making a positive contribution to the world.

In the Words

So, you enter into a space where people are embracing negative dialogue -- either about a subject, a person, religion, politics, or whatever. Do you stay and take part in that? Do you argue your point until you make everybody believe as you believe? Does your dialogue continue until you and whom ever is around you is so agitated that you end up in a physical confrontation? Or do you walk away?

You must understand that if you remain in debate, all you are actualizing is the revamping of meaningless banter and discourse. Yes, you may have your opinion, based on fact or fiction -- we all do. Yes, you may like or dislike a person who is in the spotlight, based on whatever ideology. But, as long as you are taking about them, all you are doing is adding to their notoriety. It is kind of like the fact that Andy Warhol never read the reviews written by his critics; all he did was measure how big the printed discourse was.

What this means is that you are either becoming you and becoming more. Or, you are not. If you are not -- if you find yourself constantly in verbal discourse, constantly engaged in debate, on how you feel, what you believe, or what you think about this person or that, than all you are doing is basing your life upon the actions and achievements of other people.

You can be an armchair quarterback and talk, blog, or write, (good and bad), all you want about another person or another person's philosophy. But, if you are doing this, all you are actually doing is paying tribute to that person. And, if you are following this life course, then you must ask yourself, what does it equal and how it is causing you to become more, better, and achieve what you truly desire?

So, argue if you want. Stay in the debate if you must. Hit below the belt if that is the only way you can win an argument. But, ultimately what does that say about you? And, more importantly, if you live your life at this level, what will be left when you have exited this place we call Life. Will you have left a positive legacy? Or, simply a plethora of forgotten conversations based upon meaningless opinions?

The Emotion of Emotion

On the spiritual path the concept of the human condition of emotions becomes a complicated issue. This is based in the fact virtually all of the eastern-based schools of philosophy detail that emotions are a creation of the thinking mind. As such, they are not real or valid -- simple a manifestation of the lower-self. For this reason it is taught that emotion must be dominated into submission, until they no longer exist.

With this as a basis of philosophy, for an untold number of centuries zealots have attempted to tame their emotion -- believing them to be wrong and less than holy. But, this concept must be put to the test if one truly wishes to reach the higher realms of human consciousness.

The first thing that we must look at is the root of emotions. Do all humans have them? Yes. Are we born with them? Yes. Are they exhibited from our first days of life forward? Yes. Therefore, as has now been proven, emotions are a condition of life. With this being the case, by their very definition, they are an irrefutable element of human life and, therefore, cannot be overruled as some form of invalid or lower consciousness.

This being stated, there are both positive emotions and negative emotions. Whereas positive emotions are self-fulfilling, negative emotions, on the other hand, are the primary cause of human misery. Why? Because, if you are not feeling the way you want to feel, receiving what you feel you should be receiving, then the negative emotion of unhappiness is embraced. And, this emotion has the potential to not only devastate your life, but the lives of all those around you.

If we look at the concept of negative emotions from a psychological perspective, we see that it is understood that negative emotion are kept in checked by a combination of our societal programming, our conscious, and our own force of personal will. But, in each of our lives there have been moments where emotions have gotten the better of us. We have all cried over the loss of loved ones or lost hallowed possessions. We have all been made angry by the unconscious acts of others. We have all felt hurt when our emotional needs and desires have not been met. Most of us perceiver and make our way through these time periods -- feeling the emotions and then moving forward, without causing harm or discomfort to others. But, there are those, whose emotions are not in check and they act out, beyond the normal realms of acceptability, as they are unable to control their emotions.

Why do some people step beyond the boundaries of the normal exhibition of emotions? There are several reasons. Mostly, it is based in the fact that from an early age forward, the people who behave in this fashion did not develop the techniques needed to control the expression of what they were feeling. And, from this, they learned they were, in fact, able to control the emotions of other people and in some cases actually control the entire lives of others by acting out their emotional upheavals. From this, they came to gain a sense of misplaced power over others -- all be it based from a very negative perspective.

The simple fact being, yes, people will give into the whims of others when they are expressing their emotions in an overt, abnormal manner. But, this is not based in caring about the individual. Instead, it is based in the pacification of a situation -- so that the person who is witnessing this style of negative behavior can consciously move away from the person throwing the emotional fit.

Manipulation

The use of abnormal emotions is, in fact, the basis for the science of manipulation. For why does anyone want to manipulate anyone or any situation? Because they want to gain a desired result from that person or that situation. In many cases, due to the misaligned psychological perspective of the person attempting to manipulate a situation, they base their actions upon their own emotions.

It must be understood that manipulation is a very refined science. The fact of the matter is, however, many people who have developed the ability to use manipulation as a tool to achieve their own psychological ends, do not ever understand what they are doing or how they are achieving it, they simply have come to understand that by acting in a certain way, saying certain things, they will get their desired end result. Some, on the other hand, are very aware of what they are doing and how they are doing it. For this reason, you must remain very conscious when you are dealing with an individual who bases their life upon emotional manipulation.

Anger and cruel words is an obvious tool of manipulation. It is learned very early in life that if you behave in an angered manner, in many cases, you will be able to take control over a situation and get what you want. This is the primary tool that parents use in the control of their young children. And, this is the source-point for where this style of emotional manipulation is learned.

People who were subjected to parents who were very verbally and physically demeaning of their actions, their looks, or their choices, during their childhood, are also those who were schooled, from a very early age, to use the manipulation of anger. It is very common that by criticizing a person, *"Putting them down,"* if you will, that person will be manipulated into accepted the desires of the person who is unleashing the negativity. This too, is based in the fact that many people, during their young lives, were indoctrinated into a belief system that they should make people in a position of power happy. And, by an individual saying demeaning words to a person, they are hoping to establish themselves into a position of power over another. But, it is you, who will or will not allow this happen.

Emotional manipulation also becomes a much more refined science when it is employed from the other end of the spectrum; i.e. compliments. At its most rudimentary level, people who are courting are using emotional manipulation, *"You are beautiful." "I love your hair." "I love your eyes." "You make me feel so special."* But, more than simply the obvious levels of this style of manipulation, people use much more refined techniques of emotional manipulation. For example, they many compliment what a person has achieved, or how impressive it was that they overcame specific obstacles in their life. Or, from an even more refined perspective, they describe a person's life to them as if it were a tale of great worthiness. However the manipulation card is played, manipulation is simply used as a tool to gain a desired dominance over the person. This dominance may be wanted for any number of reasons: friendship, sex, financial gains, access to people or position, etc. But, at its root, it is based in one thing, emotion. And, emotion, used in this manner, is a destructive element on the pathway to elevated consciousness. This is true for the person using it and for the individual who buys into the manipulation.

The question can then be ask, *"What should one do when they find themselves in the realms of manipulation?"* There are several things you can do. One, you can just walk away. Two, you can explain to the person that you see what they are attempting to do. Three, you can observe what they are doing, from an enlightened perspective, and simply let them play out their life melodrama while not becoming engulfed in what they have to say. The choice is yours. But, what is essential is that you do not fall prey to their techniques of manipulation, no matter how refined they may be.

Verbal Conflict

Similar to those who use manipulation, the case of people who intentionally start verbal conflicts are also attempting to take control over a situation or another person's life by the use of emotion. Certainly, we have all encountered people like this. People who attack with words and agitation at a moments notice over the most benign subjects or passing statements. They feel that what another person is saying or feeling is rudimentarily invalid. From this, they feel they have the right to express their emotion in the most violent manner possible.

Now, whatever psychological motivation: a bad childhood, a bad adulthood, or an unhappy life may spawn this type of behavior in a person, it does one thing and that is to attempt to make everyone they encounter uncomfortable. In essence, what they are trying to do, by acting out in this manner, is they are attempting to shift and then control the emotions of those around them. They have learned that by behaving in this way, most people will simply let them rant and rave and become quite. From this, they gain a sense of misplaced power over the situation or the person.

The reality, from a spiritual perspective is, if you encounter a person like this on their playing field -- that is to say if you allow them to drag you into the argument, then they have won -- at least from their warped perspective. So, it is up to you if you want to fight or to walk away. If you fight, your emotions will be stimulated and war will equal more war. If you walk away, however, then the person is left to their own solitary mental war. Or, if you are a very focused person, you can simply let them ramble what ever it is they feel they have to say, laugh it off, and move along on your own life-path. Your choice...

The Emotion of Emotion

You see, we live an emotion-based existence. And, the emotion of emotion is one of the primary motivating factors for all forms of human activity. Most people are so lost in nursing their emotional well-being at all time, however, that the majority of people do not understand the true essence of emotion -- emotions are emotional.

Vivid emotions, particularly negative emotions, cause your blood pressure to rise, hormones to race through your body, and your heart rate to increase. From this, you become stimulated. This emotional stimulation can become very addictive. And, this addiction is what separates the uncontrolled emotions of the average person from the emotions of those who walk the spiritual path.

It is certain that we all have encountered situations that have upset us. It is also certain that we have all sat around and thought about those situations, reliving and rethinking them. From this, all of those negative emotions were relived and our bodies and mind were pumped full of negative stimulation -- though it was negative, it was very stimulating.

What happens with people who embrace a life based in negative emotional encounters is that they become addicted to the sensations attached to these encounters. From this, they go out and recreate similar situation that will give them the fix of their drug of choice -- negative emotion.

What is the answer? Emotions are natural. They are a byproduct of life. They cannot be alleviated. If they could be, then monks would have found a way to do so many generations ago. As we cannot separate ourselves from emotions, we should not try. But, as people walking the pathway to higher consciousness what we can do is to understand the basis of emotions and know that they are an integral part of us. Knowing and accepting this, we may then chart a course for our lives that embraces the positive aspects of emotions and keeps us separated from the control hands of negative emotions and those who do not understand the true essence of existence.

Let go of the negative. When it is encountered, witness it but do not become controlled by it.

What you feel is your choice.

Choose your emotions. This is Zen.

The Rules Are For Sissies

Have you ever noticed how strong and bold people are when they are in a group or when they are hidden behind a cloaked of anonymity? During these conditions they are able to do all kinds of things that makes them feel empowered and makes them appear as if they are a part of the greater good. But, get them alone, expose them for who they are, and all of sudden they become very weak and very docile.

This is the problem when people are not defined by a true sense of self, are not strong in who they are, and do not have a true sense of self-assurance. For a person who is self-security is able to stand up alone and fight the most daunting opponent. Those who are weak hide behind groups and anonymity.

This mindset of weakness is also illustrative of mob mentality. When there is a group supporting the person, egging them on, then they will push forward with their position. But, the moment they are alone, they again must hide behind nicety and secrecy for they are not strong enough to stand their own ground and go face-to-face with a person.

People like this are just sissies.

Follow the Leader

Throughout time, people have followed leaders that guide people towards disaster. Why do people follow? Because they are feeble minded and due to their weakness of mind, they find that if they follow the rules and join in with the crowd then, somehow, they may be accepted and become someone who matters. But, anyone who follows the rules of any person, organization, or movement is not a true person and is not whole unto themselves. They do not know true-self, they only know how to follow. And, a follower never becomes a leader. They are simply damned to a life of continually tying to gain a sense of self worth by following the guidelines of others.

Certainly, we can all understand that one who follows another person or a group into a lifestyle that commits crimes, knowingly hurts people, and eventually lands in jail is not a good thing. But, how is the person who follows the rules of a group that promises what they are doing is righteous any different?

What is righteous? Righteous is only the consensus of whatever group is preaching its virtues. It does not make what they are teaching universally right or good. It is just what a group is programmed into believing by the, oftentimes, charismatic leader of the group.

So, anyone who follows this path of so called righteousness and goodness is nothing more than a pawn. And anything that they do is nothing more than following a pathway that has no true fulfillment at its end. Why? Because in all cases, groups, polices, ideologies, and rules change. Then, the person who has followed them, supported them, and been guided by them becomes nothing more than the garbage that is tossed away once the structure for the group is no longer a valid platform. Moreover, any person who has followed the path of the group, be it so-called good or bad, positive or negative, has done nothing but created bad karma for themselves, because they have negatively affected and, in some cases, actually hurt the lives of the other people they have accosted while they were walking the path, founded by the group consciousness.

A clear way to come to understand if what you are doing is wrong, when you believe it to be right, is to simply ask yourself, *"Who are you doing it for?"* And, *"Why are you doing it."* If doing it makes you feel better, more fulfilled, part of the greater good of a specific group, or you think what you are doing will somehow put you in better standing with the group, then you are living a lie of consciousness. You are not whole onto yourself. You are simply a small-minded follower attempting to find self worth from those you are giving your power to. Plus, if you believe that what you are doing is following the rules and, therefore, you have somehow become more or better as you chastise, criticize, physical or mentally hurt or damage another person, then you are simply delusional. As you are delusional, you have proclaimed yourself to be very weak. And, from weakness, based in negativity, you can never become strong.

Face facts; if you damage anyone, at any level; if you attack anyone at any level, you are cultivating bad karma and it will come back to haunt you. It is as simple as that.

If you think you are following the rules, written in, *"The Rule Book,"* of the group or helping the group to become better by doing what it is that they ask you to do, you are still developing bad karma. Just because something is sanctioned by a group does not make it pure or right.

Rules only exist to get the people at the top of the heap what they want. By creating rules, the people at the top fill their own egos by having people do what they want them to do.

But let's look at life -- there never is any absolute right; just as there never is any absolute wrong. Right and wrong are only a perception of time, culture, and the mindset of those around you.

Rules are a lie. Making other people conform to the rules you believe in is a sin. And, anything that you do to attempt to get people to follow the rules, (of whatever group you belong to), will only cause you to create negative karma for yourself, which will come back and haunt you.

Whatever you do, will be done to you. It may not be today or tomorrow but it will happen. Think about it…

They Love You and They Hate You

Ever since I first began writing articles, books, and making films I have found that there are all kinds of people out there who draw conclusion about my life - who I am and what I am. Some even make up lies or half-truths about their relationship to me. Some of these people love me. Some of them hate me. But, the reality is, I have never met most these people and they do not know me or understand who I truly am -- at all.

From their beliefs, some people find reasons to criticize what I create and denounce me as human being. While others find reason to praise all that I do. And, I have seen fanatics on both sides of this issue.

Some people do all kinds of things that they think I will like, while others do all they can to destroy me. And, all of these actions are based upon some abstract rationale that they have made up in their own mind. It has nothing to do with me.

They do not actually know what I like or what I need. Nor do they know what will or will not hurt me.

Now, I am not just writing this for myself, because everybody's life is like this. The reason I reference myself is because I can access my own experiences. But, your life is no different. There are people around you who want to help you and will do anything that they can for you. Then, there are also people around you are busy talking behind your back and doing things that can make your life uncomfortable.

The question has to be asked, *"Why do people behave in this manner?"* There are a million psychological reasons… But, I think what is perhaps the most obvious is that people are not content in their own life. As they are not content and fulfilled, then they move away from their SELF and try to step into the world of other people to provide meaning to their own existence.

Why do they behave in this fashion? They may hold unfulfilled desires. They may have jealousies towards the accomplishments of others. Or, maybe they just want to hurt somebody to attempt to bring that individual down to their level of misery and unconscious existence -- because this gives them some abstract sense of empowerment.

Obviously, this previous critique is geared mostly towards those who wish other people ill-will and who are attempting to bring them down by whatever method is at hand. But, those who are obsessed with HELPING a person are equally embracing a lack of SELF. Their motivations are obviously quite different, as helping is seen to lead to the betterment of the world. But, when does helping become hurting?

In my life there have been people who have gone far out of their way to do things for me. Things that I never asked them to do. And, though they saw these actions as positive, they, in fact, ultimately damaged my life. So, the pathway to helping in never clear unless it is asked for. And, this is one of the main things that you must question of yourself before you set on a path of doing something for another person, *"Will what you do actually be seen as a gift or will it become a curse?"*

The Greater Good

I find that perhaps the most telling factor of this style of DO-ing behavior lies in the misguided logic of people who believe that what they are doing, be it positive or negative, they are doing for *The Greater Good.*

The concept of *The Greater Good* is as abstract as life, Zen and spiritually itself - because there is no clear definition of *The Greater Good*. What is good to one person is not good for another. So, saying, *"I am doing good,"* should never be used as a personal justification for this style of action. Because what you are doing may ultimately lead to a negative outcome -- even if you did not mean for this to be the response.

And, if you knowingly are doing something that you understand will negatively affect another person, and claiming it is for *The Greater Good,* your logic is misplaced because negative is always negative -- there can be only one outcome and overall culmination of that action. In fact, if you consciously unleash this type of activity on another person or persons all your actions will do is to set a course of events into motion that will come back to haunt you as all negative actions do. And, karma is never bound by time. So, though you may not feel the reaction to the action right away, sooner or later, you will experience the repercussions.

The Simple Reality

What people choose to DO is based on a simply reality -- people like what they like and they do not like what they do not like. From this is born a mindset of individual definition. I like what I like!

I like you. Because I like you, I love everything that you do.

I don't like you. Because I don't like, I hate everything that you do.

We have each met people that we like and we have met those that we do not like. That is human nature. But, this mind-stuff is not a justification for doing anything for or to another person. It is just mind-stuff. This is not a conscious basis for DO-ing.

Flip the Coin

The other side of this issue is that people commonly turn down a request to help somebody, because they feel that they do not want to do that THING the person requested. Or, they believe that doing it would not be to that person's benefit.

This leads us to the ultimate reality about giving and doing, whether asked for or not. *"How do you know what another person truly wants or needs? How do you know what you give, or won't give, will ultimately effect someone else's life?"* The reality is, you don't know.

So, before you DO -- ask. And, if you are going to DO bad things to another person, even if your actions are based upon your belief that you are doing it for *The*

Greater Good, you are lost. And, the lost are not righteous in any manner. All that they do is to bring more negativity into their own life and the world around them by choosing not to change. Don't DO bad things to people, no matter what your rationale.

Finally, ask yourself, *"Is what you are doing bringing you pride or joy?"* If it is, that makes it an ego-filled action. Ego-filled actions are not pure. Ego-filled actions only lead to negative karma because they do not come from a pure source. As they are not pure, they cause karma. And, as discussed, negative karma is not bound by time.

Think before you DO.

What's The Point of Reading Books?

What's the point of reading books if you haven't gone to the source and found out the basis of culture and mindset for where those books were written?

It is very common for people of the modern world to be drawn to a specific mindset: be it spiritual, political, or cultural. Once they develop this fascination -- which may come from any number of sources, they then go out and buy book after book on the subject, filling their thinking mind with the words written upon those pages. From this, they then believe that they have an actual understanding of what is being taught in those writing.

Quite simply, they are wrong.

People love to debate, discuss, and philosophize about subjects that they are interested in. There is a certain mindset, to a specific style of personality, who feels that they know all and that the opinion they develop, about a specific subject, is the only one that is right.

Some of these people become great orators, skilled conversationalists, and pretty much win any debate they enter, either by impressing their point upon the fragile mind's of those people they are talking with or simply by bullying their way through the conversation to get their point across.

On the other hand, some people love to learn. As such, they believe that their must maintain an open mind in order to allow each person to express themselves. From this, they believe that they may possibly learn from what another person is saying.

In either of these cases, one must ask what is the source of the knowledge that it being disseminated? Where has the person who is talking, gained their wisdom?

It must be understood that most people do not possess first-hand knowledge. They may have been taught what they are speaking about in school, read about it in a book, or perhaps heard it from someone else. Though they may believe the point of view they are presenting -- that belief does not make it a valid, actual, or universally true fact. It is simply an opinion that they are presenting.

This is the birthplace for problems.

People present their opinions as facts. But, these opinions have no bases in reality and are certainly not universal truths. They are simply opinions.

As stated, some people are great orators and they influence other people to believe as they believe. But, if what they are detailing is, *"Borrowed Knowledge,"* something not based upon personal realizations, then what they are speaking about is not founded in truth.

What is opinion? Opinion is a personal preference based in cultural, socioeconomic, and personality based reality. Thus, it is personal not a universal truth.

How often have we each heard people discussing their opinions. We see this on television, read it in magazines, in books, and witness it in coffee houses all the time. But, what do the people who express their opinion actually know? With very few exceptions, they know nothing. Their entire reality is based upon speculation and programming. And, they are too small-minded to even realize this.

Every culture on this planet breeds a particular mindset of opinions based in its cultural and religious ideologies. As the planet has become smaller, and information is more readily available, hearing about an opinion or philosophy possessed by another culture has become more and more available. Combine this with the fact that most people, as evolving individuals, at some time, become bored or dissatisfied with their own cultural philosophy. From this, many decide that the allure and the promises of another culture's opinions has much more to offer and is much more appealing than the one that is currently possessed. So, people read about this culture and the new cultural philosophy, they talk about it, and go to lectures. But, though they may study it, they do not live it.

Since the dawning of the new age, where western minds turned to the ideologies of the east, many westerners have believed that all that is holy can be found in some far off land like India. Have you ever been to India? Have you ever witnessed the poverty and the violence that is everywhere? Most people have not. Yet, they still hold fast to their belief that India is the source of spirituality.

Then, there are those who dismiss this fact or explain it away. They say, *"Well, if you look for the spirituality under the surface of their society, you will find it."* Or, *"It was very spiritual place in ages gone past."*

But, ages gone past, are ages gone past. They are not now. This is now. And, *"Under the surface,"* is an excuse or a justification, not a reality.

Which brings us to the point. If you haven't lived it, you don't understand it. No book can give you knowledge. Only living it can give you knowledge.

You may learn from a book what you do or do not want to try to experience. But, do not mistake that the words written in a book are the absolute source of truth. They are not. Mostly, they are just opinions.

This is the same for those who speak their mind. Have they lived what they discuss? And, just because they may have travel to a place, does not mean that they have lived the reality of a culture. And, furthermore, just because someone else has done something, does not mean that you too can live it -- as each person's karma is universally different.

So, put down the pages. Stop listening to the loudmouths. And, live.

Living is where the truth is born.

It Takes Two to Tango: Conflict on the Spiritual Path

When one thinks about the spiritual path, conflict is never the first thought that comes to mind. In fact, just the opposite. Conflict seems a distant concept to the spiritual practitioner. And, in many ways, this is true.

Conflict, however, is one of the defining elements of human life. And, though one may walk the spiritual path, they too must learn how to deal with it, in an appropriate and conscious manner, when it comes knocking upon their door.

Think about it, no one is free from conflict. Many of us have seen the smuggled out news footage of the violence unleashed against monks in Burma (Myanmar). And, we have heard the stories of what the Chinese military has done to Tibetan Buddhist monks and believers. I, myself, have see sadhus and yogis beaten by police in India. And, on a much smaller scale, I have seen spiritual brothers and sisters, in various states of physical and verbal conflict, at spiritual centers, here in the States. So, it is just a simple reality -- we are human, there will be differences of opinions, there will be anger unleashed based upon a person's individual psychology, and there will be confrontations. It would be great if this wasn't the case but this is simply a fact of this world.

How then, should we, as spiritual people, handle these situations when they occur?

As each situation is defined by it own set of parameters, we can discuss a few examples, so that you can hopeful have some Thought-Tools about the various types of encounters, so that when you encounter a conflict situation, you may know best how to handle it.

The Spiritual Perspective

I remember I was in Southern India, Tamil Nadu to be exact, many years ago, and this one devotee was talking to me about what would happen if a person ever accosted him with a gun. He exclaimed, *"Lord Shiva would simply make it disappear."* As I was still very young, and the memories of my adolescence were close at hand, I could not help but question his reality.

Defined by the fact of where I grew up, my childhood and adolescence were highly defined by random, and ongoing, acts of violence. Due to the intensive gang activities of the neighborhoods of my youth, I frequently witnessed gangs beating up one person, killings, and even friends stabbing friends over the most meaningless disagreements.

You see, this is one of the primary problems of the spiritual path; it feeds people a lot of illusion(s) about the realities of life. Certainly, as someone who walks the spiritual, you are far less apt to attract confrontation and/or violence. Why? Because you are consciously living in a space of conflict avoidance. As the old saying goes, *"You are what you eat."* This being stated, as previously discussed, we have each seen and heard about monks being attacked. So, simply being holy is not enough to keep you from conflict.

Another key component of the spiritual path is the concept of, *"Karma."* When something bad happens, it is just written off as, *"That was your karma."*

This is all just ridiculous nonsense. It is simply a way to justify the random acts of life and place them into some context where they may be discussed and attributed to God or the ways of the world.

But, instead of simply buying into all of the justifications for conflict and applying inappropriate reasons for why things happen, we must learn to look at conflict from a new and more WHOLE perspective. From this, not only may certain conflicts be avoided but also the ones that do take place may be understood from a more conscious perspective.

People Are People

At the root of all conflict is the desire of an individual. All conflict is based upon the simple fact that a person wants a situation to happen in a specific manner. When it does not, they become upset. Some people are conscious enough to simply realize this fact and understand that the particular situation in question is not going to turn out the way that they hoped -- they realize this, take note of it, and move on. Others, however, who live their life from a very unaware perspective and base their existence upon achieving their desired ends, by any means possible, will create conflict when things are not going their way.

Now, this happens on all different levels. For some when they are not happy with a particular situation's outcome, they become sad or depressed. Others become very hard to get along with. Some become angry and throw a fit. Others still, become violent.

Ultimately, you must understand that all of these individual reactions are a choice.

It is you who chooses how to behave in any given situation. It is also you who chooses how to behave when someone is encountering you with a conflict-based mindset, based in the fact that his or her individual desires are not being met.

Anger

An example of this happened to me early into my immersion into the film industry -- when I was creating one of my first feature films. I had invited this guy to come onboard and help me produce the movie. We had several cast and crewmembers at our downtown Los Angeles location.

Now, it must be understood, on a film set, there can be only one captain of the ship. Though you have people helping you on many levels, there can be only one guiding force or a project becomes convoluted.

On this day the shooting was progressing and we had planned to meet up with this one, non-actress, girl that my associate was infatuated with and wanted to put into the movie. Though I was happy to have her in the movie, I had a realization that due to time and location constraints we should wait until the next day to use her because I realized that we could shoot her character's scenes at a much better location. I explained this to him and he completely freaked out. He started yelling and screaming -- which ultimately upset my cast. One has to question, where does this kind of reaction come from? Because most people would not react like this. They would simply understand and readjust their thinking.

Where it comes from is a very childlike mind-space. A place where, as a child, this person learned that if he yelled and screamed long enough, he would get what he wanted. In fact, this type of behavior is very common. Many adults use it. And, in some cases they do get what they want. In other cases, like the one I am describing, this person's behavior simply made everyone one else ill at ease by his actions. But, it must be understood that in some cases that is exactly what a person wants -- to take control over a situation by whatever means possible.

In regard to the film, ultimately, we did what I suggested. The movie was completed. And, the man realized that my choice of shooting the girl at a different location was, in fact, the best thing to do. But, the damage this type of behavior unleashed is never repaired.

By nature, I am a very forgiving person. So, this person vacillated in and out of my life for the next decade or so. Every now and then, however, I would see this same behavior emerging. Why? Because people are who they are.

People Are Who They Are

"People are who they are." This is one of the most important understandings to come to when studying the nature of conflict. There are certain people who avoid conflict. If you associate with them, your relationship will be relatively conflict free. Then, there are others who seek it out -- for whatever reason. If you associate with them, there will be conflict. And then, there are those who exist somewhere in between these two polarities.

Each person has the choice to react to any situation in whichever way they want. This, *"Choice,"* is based in so many elements: Biology, Sociology, and Psychology. How they were born, how they were raised, how they were indoctrinated into life, who they grew up around, what was their societal environment, etc., etc., etc. This being stated, again, people are who they are. But, few ever choose to consciously define who they TRULY are. They simply exist in the body they were given and the mindset they were indoctrinated to believe is theirs. Few ever choose to truly define themselves as a complete person. Thereby, if they are locked in a mindset of, *"Me," "That's what I want,"* or basing their existence upon generalized desire, they are at the heart of causing a conflicted world.

Friend or Foe

As I was speaking about the film industry, another revealing story about human nature affecting the realms of conflict comes to mind...

An amusing, interesting, and revealing situation occurred on one of my films.

One of my older college students, who had taken a couple of my classes and was very interested in working with me, continued to contact me. He called and he called. I finally gave in and let him come onto one of my sets.

On the first film he worked with on, he simply was the boom operator. The shoot was simply an afternoon gig and there were no problems. On my next film that he worked on, I let him shoot some of the scenes that I painstakingly set up, as he wanted to become a cinematographer. Again, no problem. On the third film, however, he had purchased a camera, had been practicing, and I allowed him to be one of the camera operators. The problems began to arise when he decided that the movie was his production -- which it was not. This was due to the fact that I allowed him to help me with casting.

Perhaps the most interesting element of this casting equation came into play when I found out that he was a professional drug dealer. I guess I should have known because several months earlier we had met at the American Film Market and he did one of those things where you shake hands and, as we did, he put some pot in my hand. I laughed and gave it back to him.

In any case, we were having a casting meeting at a Starbucks in Santa Monica, California one afternoon. The funny thing was, he had also invited one of his buyers to the meeting place. When the buyer arrived, he literally went over into the nearby bushes to make his deal. Now, as amusing as this was to my production manager and myself, this was very uncool because if he had been arrested, that would have put my production manager and myself in the path of law enforcement for something we had nothing to do with it.

I overlooked this fact and continued on with the production. On the final day of principal photography this man, apparently attempting to demonstrate his immersion into the industry to his friends, had invited a guy on the set to help with boom operation -- which was fine with me. The problem was, the guy was one of those wanta-be film industry types who have never done anything but think that they know more than you and can do everything better than you. But, I just let his negative attitude go and kept moving forward. He also invited a professional cameraman he had meet at the Apple Store. This professional cameraman had brought his own equipment. He asked if he could help with filming. *"Of course,"* was my answer.

Immediately, I saw this cameraman's prowess and put him into the primary camera position. This set the problems with ego into motions...

Combine this, with at the end of that day's shoot, a cast member asked me if I knew any one who sold pot.

Because I have long hair, I guess everyone assumes I do drugs. I do not.

But, I referred him to the aforementioned student/cameraman. As drug dealers tend to be a very paranoid bunch, this set the man into a world of denial. Combine this was the fact that the guy held some false belief that I had sabotaged some hidden deal he had made with another of the cast members. And, all this set him into a rage. Luckily, he did not bring it up until the next day.

The next day, with principal photography complete, my father-in-law, who I was very close to, (as he was one of my best drink'n buddies), entered into the last stage of his life. He was dying from lung cancer. As I drove to be by his side, I get a phone call on my cel. I answer. I hear, *"Mr. Zen..."* My student then hangs up on me. But, instead of letting it go at that, he continues to leave me voice mail after voice mail, (on my separate voice mail/pager number), telling me what an asshole I am and making all kinds of threats against me. So, there I am, dealing with all of the emotions of watching my father-in-law slowing drifting from this world, as my pager continues to buzz, fed by this man's irate and meaningless conflict based behavior. He also proceeds to call and tell all of my cast and crewmembers what a jerk I am. This, when I was the only person to ever attempt to give this guy a break in the industry and to help him out.

But, in Hollywood, and in life in general, people don't see things this way. They see themselves as the center of the universe and even if they possess minimal abilities, they expect to be treated like stars or they will create conflict. Furthermore, this is the way people who wish to instigate conflict behave. It is never enough for them to discuss their dissatisfaction solely with the particular person involved. Instead, they want to drag as many people, who could care less about the situation, into the matter as possible. From this, they gain some misplaced validity to an emotion that is based solely out of the desire(s) of their own ego.

Fight or Flight

As a lifelong martial artists, one of the most essential elements I have learned is that, just because you can kick a person's ass doesn't mean that you have to do it. And, this is one of the best definitions to hold onto when you are forced to deal with an individualized conflict like the one just described. Instead of getting in there and throwing punches, just realize the limited reality that the person who is causing the conflict is embracing. In other words, become more and rise above it and them. Because by descending to their level and beating them up, all you do is grant them a sense of validity for the way they are behaving.

How did I react to the aforementioned conflict? I just let it go and I moved on. I mean the guy had sealed himself into his own wasteland. He made his choices about how he would choose to react to life situations and there was nothing I could do about it.

The moral of this story is that we each have the ability to realize who a person is and what is their individual personality. For example, the background of this guy was, this man was in his late forties/early fifties, single, never married, and taking courses at night.

The reason I mention this is that this says a lot about his ultimate character development. It is important to note that an individual's character development is something that can clue you into possible upcoming problems with conflict. In addition, when we were out looking at filmmaking equipment, he couldn't go into a certain camera store because he had a conflict with one of the employees. He also couldn't walk past this one restaurant because of a disagreement he had with a former friend who worked there, and so on.

What was obvious is that he was a person constantly creating conflict. I observed this and yet, I overlooked it. So, it was my fault that I allowed him to cause conflict with me.

Now, this is one of the most essential details to realize about the reality of conflict

-- though you cannot protect yourself from every level of conflict, because life is too chaotic and uncertain to predict anything, what you can do is to not let a specific person, who bases their life upon conflict, into your realm of existence. When you see who a person is, and they are not living in a pure space, it is best to move along.

Though it sometimes takes time to realize a person's true personality, once you do, you must make a very conscious decision whether or not you are willing to let them into your life. By practicing this simple observation technique, you will save your life-time from a lot of unnecessary conflict.

Why Do They Do It?

The ultimate questions is why do people like the previous detailed individual, cause conflict. There are obviously a lot of reasons, but one of the primary ones is adrenaline. Adrenaline is an addictive hormone in our bodies. It accelerates our minds, our cardiovascular system, and provides us a sense of hyperawareness. It is a drug. And, just like any other drug, some people are able to take it, have some fun, and not get hooked on it. For others, this is not the case.

Some people find that in the midst of conflict their adrenaline is pumping. Though they do not make this happen, from a conscious perspective, none-the-less they come to crave this adrenaline and they discover that conflict is one of the primary sources of this drug. So, they create conflict to get high.

You Never See it Coming

One of the primary locations where conflict(s) occur is in the workplace. Though I have never had a traditional job, for any length of time, I have heard story-after-story about how bosses and superiors berate their lower level employees and shift blame to them when it is not deserved. I have heard from so many people who tell me that the workplace is one of the primary points of life changing conflict.

Personally, I had an amusing situation happen to me when I was teaching a class on filmmaking for the University of California, Los Angeles, Extension Department.

I had taught a class for U.C.L.A. Extension the previous semester. The class, itself, went well enough, and I believe the students came away with some new knowledge. In fact, one of the students became a friend and we ended up making a couple of movies together. During the class, however, I saw inside the true structure of

U.C.L.A. Extension and witnessed how flawed it was.

An ideal example of this flawed system happened when we had our class shifted from the Westwood campus to the campus at Universal Studios. There, I was to teach my students about editing. We all arrived, pay the expensive parking fees, only to find out that the individual who ran these editing suits would not let us use the equipment. While we all stood there and listened, he called up the course coordinator, at the main U.C.L.A. campus, screaming at him about even allowing us to be there. In any case, after witnessing that, I swore I would never teach for U.C.L.A. Extension again.

The next semester rolled around, however, and they asked me to teach another class. Though I did not really want to do it, we all need to make a living. So, I accepted the offer.

The first day of the class I walk in and was overwhelmed. There were over forty students in a class that was specifically designed to be taught to no more than twenty. Then, I was hit with the next news. There was only going to be one camera to use in the class. What!

In the previous class I had taught for U.C.L.A. Extension, I had ten students and two cameras. With this, there was plenty of time for each student to get hands-on experience and get a true feel for filmmaking. In this new class, however, that was going to be impossible.

I complained to the program coordinator, who was this interesting lady from France. I am using the term, *"Interesting,"* to be kind. This lady possessed one of those devil-may-care attitudes, as she was the boss, and emanated all of the all-knowing, power-fed arrogance, of her position.

After I expressed my doubts, she told me that I was a professional and I should be able to teach the class just fine. In other words, she completely dismissed any of my concerns about what the students would actually be receiving from the course. This, when the students were paying in excess of one thousand dollars ($1,000.00) to take the course. Which means, that U.C.L.A. Extension made over fifty thousand dollars ($50,000.00) from my teaching the class. Think about that for a moment...

Another interesting caveat is that U.C.L.A. Extension offers only a limited refund when a student drops a course. So, I knew there was going to be problems. But, interesting business plan, don't you think?

A few classes in, this very large, very gay female student, asks if she can bring her girl friend into the class. *"Sure, why not."* I should have known something was up...

In any case, she sits down in the front row, with her arm around her lover, occasionally giving her a kiss. Weird, for any class. But hey, I'm an opened minded guy...

About half way through the session, she erupts. There was this Armenian porn producer/gun dealer also in the class. Actually, a very nice guy. But, he was prone to speaking his mind. He said something. She exploded at him. She then exploded at me and everything went to hell. She stormed out of the room, hand-in-hand with her lover. I shook my head, smiled, and somewhat dismayed, attempted to carry on.

Who's Side Are You On?

The next day I get a call from the aforementioned French program coordinator. She tells me that the girl wanted out of the class. She wanted all of her money back. Plus, she still wanted the ability to film on the U.C.L.A. campus, with the promised camera. To achieve this end she had filed some kind of stupid misconduct charge against me for discussing the fact that there is nudity in the independent film industry. I mean, come on, who doesn't know that and hasn't seen it a millions times on the screen? Plus, she had her girlfriend to back up her charges. I realized that I had been sucked into the middle of a total set-up.

You see, this is one of the problems with modern life -- it doesn't matter if something is true or not, simply a person making the claim, has the potential to derail another person's life.

But, it was my fault. I should have seen it coming -- the high cost of the course, the too many students in one class, and only one camera. I should have walked away and not taught the class.

I explained to the program coordinator that this was at least partially her fault, as she overbooked the class to make as much money for the department as possible, and she did not provide me with the appropriate and promised equipment to teach the class correctly. Of course, she dismissed everything I said. Frustrated by not being heard, *"That's it. I quit."* I hung up the phone.

The next day I get a call from the head of the department. She put four of us on a conference call: herself, the program coordinator, the course coordinator, and myself.

I had never met her, as she was new to U.C.L.A., but she was actually a very nice person. I explained to her the situation, as the French program coordinator claimed to have not understood that there was any problems. Basically, it was so blatantly obvious, even to the head of the department, that the program coordinator was simply trying to save her own ass.

Me, I continued to state my resolve to quit. But, the head of the department was so nice that I gave in and completed the class. (She obviously did not want to refund all of that money, to all those students). The French program coordinator lied and kept her job. And I, of course, have chosen to never teach for that program again.

The U.C.L.A. powers-that-be blinked and gave in to the woman who threw the fit. She got her refund and got to shoot the final weekend of the course on the U.C.L.A. campus with a camera provided by the department. The false allegation against me were obviously dismissed. So, who won? And, what was gained by any of it?

Well, I believe the woman who stormed out of class lost out, at least on the learning experience, because she did not learn all of the secrets of the independent film industry and independent film production and distribution that I taught the class -- which is why she signed up for the class in the first place -- right? But, in the process she tarnished my reputation as an instructor.

Did I really care? No, not really. Because I knew the truth. But, that is just who I am...

I suppose if being a university professor was my ultimate goal in life, it may have matter more. Because it could have crushed my career.

The ultimate question of any conflict is, *"What do you gain and what do you lose?"* Before you engage in any conflict, you have to ask yourself, *"Why are you doing it? And, is any of it worth it?"* Plus, if you instigate one of these situations, you have to ponder what kind of karma are you creating simply to get your own way and fulfill your own momentary desires.

This is the primary problem with conflicts in general. As detailed, they are all based in a person's desires -- as momentary as they may be.

Think about it, how many of your desires have lasted for more than the moment they were felt? How much of any anger you have may have felt has lasted for more than the few moments it was experienced?

Emotions go by the wayside. This is simply a fact of life. What is felt today, will not be felt tomorrow. What you do with emotions, while they are being felt, is what defines you either as a conscious spiritual person or simply a person who bases their reality around the limited perceptions of the world.

Moving On

The next semester I taught at Santa Monica College -- a much more laid back environment. In the first class of the session I was speaking to a student and she said, *"I don't know how you can teach, everybody is always out to get the teacher."* I smiled.

You see, this is life. There is going to be conflict and it is going to come at you from a direction you never expect. Conflict can happen, even when you are trying to do a good thing and a good job. Why? Because, people only care about themselves and their own momentary reality. And, they are willing to do whatever it takes to fulfill whatever desire they have in that moment. Plus, they could care less what effect what they are having on the life of another person. As you now see, it even happens to me.

So, what is the answer? Just as with the examples I have given you -- had I listened to my inner-voice, the conflict would never have occurred. Had I listened to my inner-voice and either not chosen to interact with a specific individual or allowed myself to be put in a less than ideal environment than I would not have gone through the experience. Furthermore, had I just walked away, once I could see that the situation was going South, then the ultimate conflict orientate outcome would not have occurred. So, the main point in avoiding conflict is you really have to trust your inner-voice and not put yourself in situations where a conflict is waiting to happen.

In the fighting ring and on the chessboard, the first rule is to unleash a powerful offense. The basis for this is that you want to take your opponent out with a rapid and precise first-strike. Though few people who instigate conflict know this rule, this is what they are doing. They hope by creating a crisis that they will defeat their opponent before they even have the chance to compete. But, here is the secret to defending against this style of offense -- do not compete.

If you do not care about the outcome of a conflict, than how can you be dragged into it? If you do not care, you will not argue or fight to win. Just like with the previously discussed examples, the movies were being made with or with out these problematic people. So, why would I care if they participated or not? It was out of my kindness that I offered them the opportunity to come on-board. Regarding the teaching assignment -- I didn't want it anyway. I was the one offered the position, and I accepted it solely as a means of helping the students. So, if I never went back, who cares? Not me.

This is the mind-space you must live your life from. You must orchestrate your reality to live in a space of refined consciousness. You do what you do, and hopefully you can help some others in the process. But, never put yourself in a position where you must rely upon others. By living your life from this perspective you are free and you will never be drawn into a conflict.

People

People each have their own life, lifestyle, and psychological makeup. They each have the potential to come at you, cause conflict, and mess up your life in ways you never expected. This can easily derail anything you are working towards. So, you really have to be careful whom you bring into your life and where you place yourself in this Life-Space.

Trust your feeling and if you are getting weird vibes from a person, (or if a crewmember is making drug deal during a casting meeting or a student brings her girlfriend to class and puts her arm around her), steer clear of them as they have the potential to mess up your life. Move away, move on. And, if you find yourself engulfed in a conflict situation, it is far better to nip-it-in-the-bud, close-it-out, and walk away before it ever has the potential for escalation.

No One Wants Success
They Just Want to Know How Much They Are Getting Paid

Everywhere you look, there is some book, some CD, some training course about how to become successful. Though the authors and the presenters of these books and courses may be considered financially successful -- due to the fact of their getting paid for the subject; the people who read these books, listen to the tapes, and take the courses are generally far from it.

Why is this? Because people don't want success, they simply want to get paid.

To elaborate, the world society is based upon financial wealth. If you have enough money, it is believed that you can buy whatever you want, be is things, people, happiness, and health. And, in certain regards, this is true.

Think about this, how many well-known and famous, politically or spiritual pundits, hang around with poor people? Very few. Why? Because unless they are using a, *"Poor Person,"* for some form of Public Relations (P.R.). That, *"Poor*

Person," serve no purpose. There is nothing that they can do for them.

The other side of the issue is that money does not buy everything. Think about how many rich and famous people have committed suicide, are drug addicts, (both via a doctor's prescription and otherwise), or have gone through years of therapy due to the fact that they are mentally unstable.

This being stated, it doesn't change the fact that people want to get paid. They believe that simply because they are who they are, they deserve to get paid.

As an independent filmmaker, where the production budgets are commonly very tight, I have addressed this issue to numerous people and in a number of articles and books. As I have explained, *"Your name is not going to sell any copies of this movie. What I am offering you is, no money, but the opportunity to be in a feature film which is a steeping-stone to helping your career."* Some have understood this and have taken part in a film. Which, in many/most cases was the only film they were ever in. Others, thinking that they will be, *"A Star,"* tomorrow, have not. Of these people, none of them were ever seen or heard from again. They certainly were never in any film.

You see, this is the simply truth about reality and the pathway to success. Success is not measured in how much you get paid. Success is measured in what you have accomplished.

Plus, if what you accomplish is positive and leaves a positive impression on the world, then the world becomes a slightly better place. For those who seek out negative actions, and do negative deeds, the opposite is true.

Let's take a moment and ponder this. In your life, when have you felt the most fulfilled? Was it when you were doing something that you did not want to do but where being paid money for the activity? Or, was it when you were pursuing something that you really wanted to be doing -- something that made you, and hopefully this place we call life, just a little bit better?

The answer is pretty obvious. But, this is where the problem arises. People get confused about their own self worth, (what they are worth, monetarily), and what they are doing with this life.

In this world-society, celebrity seems to be the ultimate goal. Because with celebrity comes fame, fortune, admiration, and riches. And, this is not only the case in the realms of traditional celebrity: such as acting, writing, and the arts. It is in the spiritual realms, as well.

Think about how many, *"Famous,"* spiritual teachers there are. The problem is, because they are, *"Famous,"* they are accepted as being all-knowing, righteous, and virtuous.

But, I think from recent news reports, we all now know that being, *"Famous,"* in the realms of spirituality does not necessarily equal universal goodness. In fact, just the opposite. Many spiritual teachers have used their positions to gain control over the body, the mind, and the finances of those who follow them.

But, why follow anybody at all? Many who follow a particular church or person, believe that the group or person, and what they teach, is holy or is motivating. They believe that what the teacher has to say is meaningful and gives them guidance. That's all good. But, that is not the end-all to life. That simply means that they are saying something that you want to hear. That is, until the person does something that you find unholy or unjust and you leave them behind.

Again, this entire situation is based in the quest for fame and the money it provides. Does a swami, a priest, or a motivational speaker have an ego. Of course, they do. Those professions walk hand-in-hand with the promises of ego gratification. Sure, they can claim and pretend to be holy. That too makes them gain more flock. But, it all equals the same thing. A person is a person is a person. Some were trained or simply provided with the personality and temperament at birth to teach.

In life, we each make our choices. What it is we will do with our Life-Time based upon the availability of choices that surround us, is up to us. So, we make our choices from the available options and then pursue our passions, to whatever degree.

Now, here arise the problem and the focal-point of this essay. We are all formed and shaped by what we see, what we experience, what we perceive is good and/or bad, and what we want. Due to the fact that in this modern world we are bombarded by fame, celebrity, and power. It is believed that each of these are the pathway to equaling the wealth that we perceive will allow us to live the lavish or obtaining the all-that-we-want lifestyle.

And, think about it, how far each person goes after it, is entirely based on individual determination.

Most people have very little determination. They may want to be a movie star, a sport star, a rock star, a political figure, a business owner, or a priest, but they do not have the focused dedication to follow through with obtaining that dream. This is where the people who market *"Success,"* come into play. For, those who hold desires to be something else/something more are the people who buy the books and attend the seminars. They are the people who want to, but the people who do not have the dedication to obtain.

This brings us back to the point of, *"Getting paid."*

People hold onto the belief that, *"Someday,"* they will be what they desire. And, that if they have taken a small step in the direction of obtaining their goal -- whether it be taking a class, learning how to play an instrument, learning how to throw a football, wearing a certain style of clothing, or simply believing that they are pretty-enough, they should then be paid the minute they show up on the scene. What will this money equal to them? Validation. A sense that they have arrive. A feeling that they are good enough. That they are walking the right path. That they, *"Knew it." "I am somebody!"*

This is a condition of our world society. It is not, however, a condition of truth.

People who live in the world of desire, of seeking, of obtaining, or gaining, are locked into a path of being judged. Though they may think that they are good enough that does not mean that they are. Though they may be good enough today, that does not mean that they will be good enough tomorrow.

Think about the actor you saw in a movie once and then never saw again. Think about the singer who had one great song. Whatever happened to them? Think about the football star who got hit in the knees and their career was over. Think about the model that got old. Think about the restaurant owner whose clients went away. The business owners whose product was no longer needed. The minister with no church. And so on...

If you choose to live a lifestyle where you are judged, you will forever be judged. You will be judged whether you are good enough or not.

If you doing what you are doing and expecting to be paid for it, the question will always arise, are you worth the fee?

Think about it. What are you doing? And, why are you doing it. What are you pursuing? And, why are you pursuing it?

Simply question. You should have an answer.

Paying For Your Sins

It is always an interesting concept about the way people justify the negative actions of others. This is particularly the case when something bad befalls a person. *"They got what they deserved,"* are the words that are commonly spoken. Or, *"They have gotten their karma."*

Now, it is all very well-and-good when a person who has done something wrong encounters a negative experience of his or her own. In some ways it does appears as if they are getting what they deserve. But, the concept of karma and retribution is far more complicated than all that. Moreover, so is the concept of actually paying for your sins.

Reviewing the Concept

The first thing to understand when reviewing this concept and the, *"What goes around, comes around,"* mentality is that, let's face facts -- most people do not believe that what they are doing is wrong. The wrongness of their actions is only seen by others who are witnessing it or have heard about it from others.

People, on the whole, are very selfish, self-centered creatures. They believe that whatever is right for them, whatever makes them feel good, or whatever makes their life better, is the only criteria from which they are judged.

Think about this. Why do you do what you do? In most cases, it is to make your life better, more happy, more fulfilled, give you more money, a better lifestyle, get you the possession that you want, get you into bed with the person you desire, or whatever. And, the sad truth is, whatever you are doing to make your life better, more happy, more fulfilled, or richer, you could care less about the effect your actions are having on others.

The reality of humanity is, people do not care and rarely even think about what effect their choices and their actions are having on others. All they care about is whether they are getting what they want out of whatever it is they are doing.

Bad Behavior

People knowingly lie, cheat, and deceive others to gain whatever it is they desire. In addition, they do not care what impact their actions have on people, society, culture, or the environment.

Think of every used car that is sold. Why is somebody selling it? Because it needs work. Do most used car sales men mention this? No they do not. All they talk about is what the used car has to offer.

Think of every time you have gone into a store and have received the hard-sell from an employee. Why do they do this? Because they are working for a commission. Which means, they must sell you something, to make money and they do not care how the sale may negatively affect your life. All they care about is making money.

Why do people lie? Because they want to appear to be something more than what they are. Because they want to appear as if they have some possession, some knowledge, that others do not possess. Why? Because they want people to like them. They want to be revered and desired.

Why do people bad-mouth you? Because they want somebody to like them more than they like you. Because they want somebody to dislike you because they dislike you. Because that want to appear as if they are more than you.

These are just four examples. If you take a moment, you can think about a million more.

Plus, if you add up all of the things that people physically do to others from beating them up, to stealing from them, to breaking or damaging their property, the list of, *"Bad Karma,"* activates becomes virtually incalculable.

The Primary Reality

The main thing to realize is that this style of behavior and action travels into other areas of life, as well. But, whatever the causation factor, whatever the reason, all of these actions equal one thing -- hurting and taking away from the life of other people.

There is one primary reality here. And, this is something that most people never even think about. What they are doing is hurting others to gain what they, personally, desire.

Selfish Reality

This all being said, most people are so locked into their own, *"Selfish Reality,"* that they do not even care what affect they are having on other people. This is generally the case, until something bad happens to them.

When something bad happens, the first thing that people generally do is to blame the person who inflicted the action on them, blame life, blame god, blame society, whomever... But few people ever blame themselves.

Those who do, those who begin to see that there is karma involved, that they may be paying for their past actions, then tend to pray and ask for forgiveness. But, how does god forgive you for what you have done to others?

Here is one of the main problems with modern religious ideology -- people turn to god for forgiveness. But, it is not god that they sinned against. It is not god that they hurt. Who they hurt, who they damaged, is another person. So, it is that person who they should be asking forgiveness from.

Caring Verse Noncaring

Now, admittedly, most people don't care. Most people go to their graves justifying their *"Life Actions,"* believe that all they did, was for a reason -- be it god-and-country, supporting their family, or simply doing what it took to get what they wanted or needed. But, this is all bullshit. This is simply people justifying their actions. It is not truth. It is not reality. And, it is not godly, on any level, to have consciously hurt anyone for any reason, be it to sell your used car, to pay your rent, to buy something that you wanted, or to get into the pants of a person you desired.

Wrong is wrong! It is as simply as that!

Now, here is where a few conscious people, (and believe me, there are very few conscious people walking on this planet), try to make amends for their negative actions.

But, why are they doing this? Why are they trying to right their wrongs?

Fixing What You Have Broken

Number one: it is not to resolve their negative karma or pay for their sins. Because if this is the case, it can never happen.

Just like if you break the cookie jar and glue it back together, it will never be the same -- trying to fix what you broken in another person's life can and will never happen.

What you can do, however, is to replace the cookie jar with a better one.

What you have to do, if you hope to remedy your past actions, is to give the person or person's you damaged something that will actually make their life better!

Number two: if you are looking for forgiveness, forget about it!

All the time we hear people stating, *"I forgive the person,"* who did a bad thing to them. This is all just verbal nonsense. It is meaningless. They do not forgive, because they cannot forget. So, saying, *"Sorry,"* means nothing. Saying, *"I forgive you,"* is meaningless.

Again, what must occur is that you must give a person you hurt a replacement for what you damaged. You must give them something that will truly help their life.

Through Your Own Eyes

Now, the problem that occurs at this stage goes back to the same root cause of why people damage people in the first place. As discussed, the majority of people do not care about other people. But, if you decided that you do care about another person or persons you then are initially seeing them through your own eyes, through your own set of desires.

For example, most of us have seen a person down on their luck and we want to help them. But, we want to give them some form of help that we believe will help them. But, this is where problems arise.

At the most obvious level, you may like a particularly style of clothing and think that a certain person, who you want to help out, who look great wearing it. But, if you buy them a new outfit or new wardrobe and they don't like that style of clothing, wearing it, will simply bring them more pain.

What this means, is that if you are actually trying to remedy what you have broken in a person's life, you have to give them what THEY want. Not what you believe they want or what you believe would make them happy.

This is where karma, and this style of paying for your sins, gets complicated. Because, if you truly wish to fix what you have broken, it may mean giving up your SELF. It may mean that you have to stop thinking about what you want at ALL levels and simply embrace what the other individual or group wants.

This is complicated. And, few people are truly willing to do what it takes to fix what they have broken -- to change the karma they have unleashed. This is why people turn to religion. Because praying to god for forgiveness, is easy. It takes nothing from the SELF.

The Rest of Your Life

But, to truly pay for your sins, fix what you have broken, change the bad karma you have unleashed, this may cost you the rest of your life. It may mean that you will need to devote your life to another person, group, or ideology, simply to buy them a new cookie jar.

Who are you ?

What have you done to gain your desires ?

What have you done to hurt others in the process ?

Do you only care about yourself ?

Are you willing to pay for your sins ?

Analyzing the Moments

How much of your life do you actually think about? How much of your life do you actually question? How much of your life, when you find yourself in a specific situation, do you actually analyze why?

If you are like most people, you never think about the reason, *"Why."* The only time you question anything is when you are truly unhappy or living a life experience that you truly dislike and you are screaming, *"Why?"*

Most people pass though their lives without ever looking at what is happening, what has happened, or ever searching out the actual reasoning for the why, of what is going on.

It is very simple; everybody wants to feel a certain way. Some people may call this fulfillment, happiness, contentment, or whatever. When they are feeling this way, they never question why. They are just feeling the way they want to feel, and they embrace it.

However, when someone is not feeling the way they want to feel or they are experiencing things that they do not wish to experience, the scream, *"Why?"* But, whom are they asking this question to? God. Maybe? But, in essence, it does not matter who or what they are asking to provide them with an answer to why they are not feeling what they want to feel. Because all they are focused upon, is the fact that they do not feel the way they want to feel.

"Why," is a revenant question. It is more an expression of discontentment than an actual inquiry. And, the question, *"Why,"* never provides an absolute answer, unless the root of, *"Why,"* is truly explored.

True Exploration are what these few word are about.

So, stop right now. Take a look at where you are, at what you are doing; what you are feeling.

It is easy to say, *"I am reading something. I am sitting in a chair. It is hot or cold outside. I feel fine."*

Again, this is all the nothingness that most people passing from birth to death would declare. But, there is a much deeper life reality than this.

Life, experience, and realization is much more profound that simply the obvious realms of reality that are going on around you. If you want to know the source, you must go to the source. You must seek it out. Perhaps most importantly, it is not that hard to do.

This time, stop, take a look at you. Truly look at this moment. And, what brought you here?

No one can give you a right answer for this. You have to give it to yourself. But, truly dig deep. Look at this moment and all the things that surround this moment. Where you are. Your environment. Your mindset. Your feelings. Your relationships. Your physical and mental reactions to even reading this book.

Take a hard look; a look that is not defined by the way you want things to be. Let your evaluation come from a sense of truth. Not from some nondescript logic of why you wish things to be different, or how you wish things to be. Simple see your reality as it is. Then, trace your reality back to its source. How did you get here?

What did you do, that equaled you being here, in this moment; being whom you are, where you are, feeling how you feel?

Once you have defined that source reality, trace it back even further. What all encompassing actions and reactions created the being, the person you are?

Now, this is not an exercise to make you feel better or worse about yourself. Because, as you will find, and perhaps already know, feeling better or worse is a temporary thing. What this exercise is designed to do is to take you back to the source. Your source. The source that caused you to be you and you to be living in this moment that you are living.

So stop, right now asking the question, *"Why?"* Instead, analyzing this moment or any moment in your life and seek out its source.

From this, you will forever find the answer to the question, *"Why?"*

Reviewing the Life and the Works of Others

It always strikes me as interesting how people go to such lengths to review the works and ideas of others. Whether this is in conversation or actually writing a lengthy review of how they feel about what another individual has created.

Everywhere we turn, we can hear people discussing what they feel about this book, that movie, a song, political or religious ideologies, or the lifestyle that a particularly individual is living.

Think about it... Do you do this?

If you do, you really need to question your motives.

Opinion

When we listen to or read the reviews that people are placing on the works of another, there is always one common thread -- opinion. At the root of any discourse is, *"I like this,"* or, *"I don't like that."* Though in truth, many people very cleverly cover up this fact.

What commonly happens is that a person goes into a subject, be it a book, a movie, music, or a discourse on a person's life with a preconceived set of ideas. In other words, they already know what they like or what they don't like. So, they enter the subject seeking a desired outcome. This means that they begin their quest either wanting to find something good, or more likely, something bad with a particular work.

Most of this behavior is based it what I called, *"Borrowed knowledge."* Which means, that anything a person is stating is based upon what they have heard, what they have previously learned from somebody else, or what they desire to be the truth.

Think about this for a moment. How much of what you believe is based solely upon what you have experienced? In the lives of most people, this is not the case. What is believed is learned from a long list of cultural and desire-based influences.

Who's Passing the Judgment?

Moreover, when you listen to or read what other's write about a subject or person, you must ask, *"Who is the person passing these judgments? Who is the person making the statement about another people and their works?"* In addition, and perhaps most importantly, *"What has the person unleashing the discourse accomplished with their life?"*

For the most part, those who issue, *"Reviews,"* particularly negative one, are those who have accomplished nothing with their own life. Because of this fact, they try to draw on the works, or the knowledge, of those who they do, *"Like,"* to find a conclusion for the claims they are making.

In discourses and reviews you will commonly hear, *"This other author said this..." "In this other book it is stated..."* Or, *"It is better to read the writings of this other person."*

What does this mean?

What it means is that the person who is casting the review is not basing their knowledge on self-knowledge, self-realization, or personally acquired understandings. What they have done is to have entered a subject with a preconceived set of ideas and then they have simply borrowed the knowledge of others to substantiate their premise.

But, the main question to ask is, *"Did the person they are quoting write the review?"* No they did not. *"Would the person they are quoting even have approved of using their name in the review?"* Probably not. Why? Because people who live a life of accomplishment do not diminishing themselves to the level of existence of critiquing others. Why?

Because they are living their life. They are creating what they create. What they are NOT doing, is basing their life upon the discussion and the review of the creations of others.

Making You a Somebody

From the dawn of evolving consciousness Self-Awareness has been the cornerstone of all metaphysical advancements. This is why we meditate. This is why we do *sadhana*. This is why we prey. Because they all lead to a refined sense of Self-Awareness. Self-Awareness is the basis of all true spirituality. But, Self-Awareness is never found in external dissemination about another person or another person's works.

It is a common belief that by writing reviews and placing them on websites, in magazines, on online discussion groups, or simply by screaming them loud enough, these actions somehow make a person a true contributor to society, *"A Somebody."* But, this is simply not the case. Why? Because what is a review? It is simply what it is, a review.

A review or a critique is not organic, nor is it a self-created work of art. It is simply discussing what another person has done or experienced, based on the reviewer's opinion.

Anyone who thinks about this will come to the same conclusion. And, for this reason, you must first analyze the motivations of a person who is writing any review or discussing another person's life. You must question why they are saying what they are saying.

A positive or negative outlook, being presented in the discussion, is a clear first-look into the motivations of an individual who is writing or saying anything. Because negativity is never based in spirituality. And, this is perhaps one of the most essential points about the Spiritual Path.

On the Spiritual Path we all must constantly review our own life. If we are looking outside, reviewing the lives and the works of others, than we are not doing this. We are simply wrapped up and playing the Life-Game. But, this is not spirituality.

If we are looking outwards, then we are not looking inwards. Outwards equals karma. Inwards equals enlightenment.

In closing, from a spiritual perspective, you must always ask yourself, *"What are you doing with your Life-Time?"* Is what you are doing making a positive contribution and helping to improve the overall positivity of this place we call life?

Or, is what you are doing simply adding to the negative melodrama by living your Life-Time passing judgment on others?

Zen is Positivity.

Zen is Creativity.

Zen is not based on critical reviews.

Zen is based on spreading the Light of Good.

What is the Light of Good? If any word in any sentence you are saying or writing is negative, then you are not embracing the Light of Good.

Ultimately life is your choice.

Do you want to be remembered as staying good things or negative things?

Good lasts forever.

Negativity is always overpowered.

Interpretation

People are continually interpreting and evaluating the works, thoughts, ideas, and expressions of other people. Interpreting and evaluating, in terms of what statement the creator of the work made, what they said, how they said it, what they did or did not do, and what they ultimately meant by it. Once the initial work in question has been viewed and judged, a person then looks to the creators other works and then to their life in order to lend credence to or dismiss what the overall message of what the individual has created. This is especially the case of writings.

Let's think about this of a moment...

Many people, throughout the centuries, have written a lot of things. All things written, or for that matter, said, are based upon an individual's personal set of experiences and understandings.

Some people truly take the time to analysis life and attempt to come to an understanding about whatever they perceive in this reality. The fact of the matter is, however, most people are not of this inclination. The majority of the world's population is simply locked into whatever momentary reality that they find themselves trapped within -- whether it be joyous or tormented.

In fact, most people don't care. They simply want to live their life and feel as good as it is possible for them to feel -- for a long as it is possible to feel that way.

An individual who bases their Life-Time upon removing as many veils from the illusion of this existence as possible, most probably will find the previously detailed individual's life very wasteful. But, the reality is, that too is a perception -- an interpretation.

Any judgment on any person or anything they have created is simply that, *"A judgment."*

Which brings us to an important point.

People interpret reality based upon a plethora of personal experiences, cultural indoctrination, and personality based understandings. And, the fact of the matter is, one person's reality can never be truly understood by another person. This is especially the case if the two individuals lived during different times in history -- even if those different time periods were separated simply by a generation or two.

For this reason, it virtually completely invalidates the interpreting of the works or the thoughts of another person if they have lived in a different time.

Religious Interpretation

This brings us to religious interpretation. From time immemorial, people have attempted to interpret the words and the works of those that are considered great spiritual teachers. But, let's face facts. Jesus didn't write the bible. Siddhartha Guatama, The Sakyamuni Buddha, did not write *The Dharmapada, The Pali Canon,* or any other work attributed to his teachings. These texts were written by others, long after the deaths of these teachers.

Were they exact replications of the words? No, they could not have been. Moreover, these writing experienced translations, interpretations, and reinterpretations, long before they ever reached the eyes of those who are reading and scrutinizing them today. By the very logic of this fact, it makes the interpretation of these writing invalid.

In the case of books such as, *The Tao Te Ching;* it is believed that it was complied by comprising several philosophic teachings and assigning it to one man, who may or may not have actually lived, Lao Tzu. Whether or not this can ever be proven or disproved, only time will tell. But, Chinese text such as these, and the ones associate with Kung Fu Tse, Confucius, have again fallen to the fate and the same process as those experienced in the Christian and Buddhist traditions. Namely, thousands of years of reinterpretations and translations.

Some people may wish to believe that the outcome they are reading was inspired by some divine intervention. But, they were, in fact, written by the hands of man. And, man, (or woman), is dominated by personal preferences and a desire for things to be expressed and come out they way in which they desire.

Again, the process makes the writing an invalid form of divine truth.

As all of these examples can be assigned to another era and another places in history, where the person who is credited with composing a book never actually wrote it, this then brings us up to the age when an author is actually the author.

With the birth of this time frame, an entire new reality of interpreting a person's thoughts, ideas, or understandings, has been born. Here/now, reviewers compare the idea(s) of one person to the thoughts and interpretations of another. Now, the thoughts of one thinker may be compared to that of another.

The problem with this style of analysis arises in the fact of the very definition of and for interpretation. Which is, *people enter any subject with a preconceived set of parameters for what they are interpreting. Each person already has a specific belief system before they begin their analysis.*

To be fair, each of us encountered thoughts and ideas in our lives that have really come to shape us. These may come in the form of words, writings, or philosophies. Wherever these sources of inspiration come from, they shape us and send us on a course that may come define the rest of our lives.

Why do certain philosophies affect different people in different ways? It is simply a case of the human condition. We each are born with a personality, which comes to define what we seek out and who we listen to in life.

This being said, it is these same elemental life-defining ideas that once they are introduced and accepted into our life, are the ones that cause us to interpret all additional information from a specific consciousness. From the point forward where our mind has been shaped, we become set in our ways and base all of our beliefs upon a predetermined set of ideologies.

Certainly, there are some people who are more open minded and accepting than others. But, those are the type of people who commonly do not unleash interpretations onto this place we call life.

The fact of the matter is, interpreted reality is, for better or for worse, the way of the world -- the way of man and woman.

So, what does this mean for you?
One, you can chose to see things in life and accept them for what they are. Be they words, writing, art, music, fashion, whatever. You may not like them. But, you exist is place of acceptance for those who think and feel differently from you.

Two, you can pass judgment.

Who passes judgment, interpreting the life and works or others? A person who wants to be seen as an intellectual or a knower. Somebody who feels they understand more than the person they are interpreting.

What they are actually doing, however, is passing judgment on another person's works. And this is the same whether they are criticizing or praising the works of that person or person(s).

Reality is based upon feelings. It is based upon how you feel about a specific subject. How does it make you feel?

This simply equation is what determines whether you will like or dislike anything.

How do you choose what you like or dislike? In many cases it is based, on a very superficial level that is determined by what information has been feed into your brain by others. This is why people join religious or philosophic organizations. This is why people believe what they believe.

But, there is something much deeper than this in life. There is a clearer, more perfect, reality. A reality where you are not influenced by the interpretations of others.

This place in you is, however, very difficult to find. That is the place in you, which is your True Self.

That place is where you are who you are. It is you.

Removed are the programmed interpretations of others that have been fed into your brain throughout your lifetime. But, more importantly, it is where you are not interpreting others. Why? Because there is no need for the interpreting of other people thoughts or ideas. Because you understand that they are. They are someone else's thoughts and realizations. They are not yours. At this place, you are one with yourself. And, no interpretation, no explanation is necessary.

Things You Will Never Know

The reality of life is that there are many-many things that you will never know or understand.

As human beings, there is the innate desire to understand. *"The how,"* and, *"The why."*

Throughout our evolution this has been the cornerstone of both realization and deception.

Realization, because it has caused us to push forward and uncover new realms of knowledge. Deception, because many false profits have capitalized upon the lack of knowledge and have claimed to know things that others do not.

The source point for all, *"So called,"* psychics are that they promise to provide people with knowledge that they wish they had but do not. This unknown knowledge can be what will happen in the future, what should somebody do next to advance his or her life, where should someone look for a desired soul-mate, or what has happened to a person who has died and what are they thinking and feeling.

In all cases, the answers that are given to these questions are dubious. Why? Because they cannot be proven or disproved. At best, they may bring the questioner a moment of peace and solace, or will guide the to person the ability to focus their intentions to the degree that they will search hard and long enough until they find what they are looking for. At worst, they will simply leave the questioning individual disillusioned.

But, here is the reality about psychics; they only exist because people what to know what they do not know. As this has been the case throughout time, psychics, by varying names and titles, have existed since the dawn of humanity.

What they promise is the same thing; answers. But, these answers are not based in truth and reality; they are based in one of two things: profit, because they are charging to provide the answers that a person wants, or control, because, by making an individual believe that they have the answers, that person is giving them the reins to guide and take control over their life.

No doubt some psychics actually believe that they have a gift. As we all have a glimmer of Divine Consciousness within us -- some believe that they have the ability to tap into Universal Knowledge.

The reality is, however, if it is True Knowledge, than not only is it freely given, it is never used to control a person. Furthermore, if it were Divine Understanding, than the person who holds such knowledge would know that all of life, is as it is. They would understand that each person knows what they need to know, is living what they need to live. And, do to this fact, all anyone can do is to live his or her own perfection. For this reason, no person should never be guided away from that path as they are embracing their own essence of perfection. And, a person's momentary desires would be seen as simply that -- momentary desire. As such, they should never be a motivation for telling someone to veer away from their own particular path of perfection.

Most *"So called"* psychics, however, go to, *"Psychic school,"* for lack of a better term. Where, it is very easy to learn how to manipulate a person by telling them certain things. As certain words and phrases easily guide a person's emotions in a very specific direction. As in all training, the more a psychic does this, the better they become at reading the variations in a person's emotions. Thus, they become masters of control.

This is also the reason most psychic readings are done in private. In this, usually dark environment, the psychic who has practiced emotional control over others, is allowed uninterrupted control over the mind of their client.

More than simply within the realms of psychic control, religion practices this same theory of domination. Religion, however, practices it over the masses. I mean, let's think about this for a moment… How many people have killed and have died it the name of religion? A lot! And, they did this, believing it was for a just cause; god.

But, more than simply interactive personal control, religion controls the minds of its followers in much more subtle ways. For example, in Christian churches, after each service, the parishioners give a donation. They are told this is to help the church. It is an offering to god. And, so on. But, what it really does is finance the lifestyle of the priest or minister.

Certainly, in this day and age, we have all heard of the bad things that certain priest and ministers have done to young devotes. So, those donations went to supporting this type of behavior.

Now, a church spokesperson might say, *"No, the money went to the church and those are just insolated incidences."* But, this is not true. Throughout history, the corruption of church official has been well documented, as have their misdeeds.

So, why does the church and/or the various religious dominations still exist? They exist because they promise answers to people who desire them. They exist because they promise a cure for people who feel that their life is empty and has no meaning. They exist because they offer forgiveness for the perceived sins of the congregation. But, who is the one that told the parishioner that what they were sinning in the first place? The church!

Here is the reality. People want to know what they do not know. They want answers to the questions that they have about life, god, reality, enlightenment, and the ever-after. But, think about it, if you simply accept that things, (that life), is as it is; you are free. If you do not peer into knowledge that does not come naturally to you -- you are also free. If you do not believe that someone else holds an answer to a question, you are free.

Here is the simple reality. No one else knows anything more than you do. Though many claim that they do. A psychic tells you that they are a psychic. They do this so they can make a living. It is their job. They tell you so they can make money off of you and possibly gain control over your life, to whatever degree. From this, they also gain a personal sense of accomplishment, and empowerment. Why? Because they have overpowered some other person.

A priest promises answers from a religion that they were programmed into believing. But, they didn't originate the religion. Thus, it is not based in organic enlightenment. It is simply borrowed knowledge.

By being a priest, they gain prestigious and power. They are provided a living by teaching and interpreting borrowed knowledge.

If you go to them for advice, they gain power over you. Thus, just as they psychic, they obtain a sense of personal empowerment. Though they may claim they are working for some supreme deity.

Again, no one else knows anything more than you.

Some may have studied how to manipulate the minds of others. Some may have studied in school or the seminar so they possess more memorized knowledge than you do. But, they do not KNOW more than you.

Anybody who says they have the answers are lying. Because you are the only person who can know you. You are the only person living your reality. So, there is no one who has the answers for you, but you.

In Your Own Moment

Since the dawning of the New Age one of the key elements has been, *"Getting into the Moment."* Terms such as, *"Be Here Now," "Get into Your Moment,"* and *"Feel Your Now,"* have been essential slogans.

This ideology, and these terms are meant to describe a sort of superior consciousness, where the individual is feeling some nondescript enhanced since of their life -- something that the average person, (apparently), does not feel.

In is common that when asked, *"What does getting into the now mean?"* Or, *"What does getting into the now feel like?"* It will commonly be described, by the pundits, as becoming childlike -- experiencing everything for the first time.

But, what does this mean? And, what are the benefits?

Somehow, in New Age, spiritual circles, it has become a type of goal to revert to a childlike mind. A mind of innocence, naiveté, and trust.

Though, from certain perspectives, these may sound like ideal qualities, there is also another side to the matter. These are the same factors that cause the child, and the child-like, to become victims of society and people.

But, more importantly, reverting in any way, is both an impossibility and an impractical desired end goal.

The reality is, each experience we have lived, each bit of knowledge that we have taken in, has contributed to who we have become.

Good or bad, all experiences have made us who we are.

To some, these experiences have lead to seeking out a spiritual mindset. Which has then guided them to seek out an understanding of living in the now.

So, what is living in the now? And, how can this be achieved?

From a philosophic perspective, living in the now means embracing each moment as a new moment. Okay, don't we all do that anyway?

Let's think about this… How are you feeling now?

The answer is, *"How you are feeling is how you are feeling."* Thus, you are already living in your now.

Many spiritual teachers and traditions believe, however, that a person should get away from their emotions. They should be removed from them, because they are somehow based in an animalistic level of human consciousness. But, are they?

As human beings, one of the essential components of our make-up is emotion. Thus, emotions are a natural state. We feel!

It is as simple as that.

You can try to hide from emotions. But, they will not go away.

And, no matter how spiritual a person claims to be, they too have emotions. As they are human, there is no way out.

This is one of the big problems when people follow teachers who are no longer alive. A dead teacher is a perfect teacher. Why? Because you will never see or experience their faults or shortcomings. All you will read or hear about is their superior consciousness. So, basically all you are exposed to is a lie. Because all living people have faults, just as they all have emotions.

Now, some people: the insane, the sociopathic, the selfish, the power hungry, and the religious zealots, for example, are driven by very negative emotions that are in complete disregard to all those around them. They do not care whom they harm to reach their own end goals. But, these are not the emotions of a normal individual.

Most of us feel happy, sad, embarrassed, frustrated, bored, in love, in anger, and all of the common emotions that are experienced throughout humanity. In terms of, *"The Now,"* these are the emotions that bring us into the now.

Think about how much of your life has passed by and you did not even notice it. Every time you ate breakfast, dinner, walked to school, drove to work, and all of the nondescript activity that make up modern life. You lived those moments, but they are gone.

Think about this… How many dinners do you remember when the food was really good, (or bad), the company you were with made you laugh and feel good, (or angry), and you were really brought to an intense emotional level? Those are the dinners you remember. The rest you do not. And, this is just one example.

Every time your emotions were turned-up, those are the time you truly remember. Those are the times you are truly in your now.

As detailed, some gurus may tell their students to rebuke emotion and live in a state of placid, meditative, abyss. But, what comes from this? What comes is a life lived with no memories -- as everything experienced is the same. Just as is the boring drive to work, day-after-day. For this, life all become a blur.

Some teachers say this leads to higher-mind. But, does it? For here is one of the ultimate illusion on the spiritual path, *"Doing nothing leads to something. It leads to enlightenment."* Or, *"A silent mind is nirvana."*

This is all the mumbo-jumbo of teachers who have not lived the enlightenment they speak of. Teachers who frame their teachings upon the borrowed knowledge of those who have walked before them. Teachers who want to control their flock and keep them silent and mindless.

Think about this... One of the key components of Zen is to become Mind-Less. For only there, some level of supreme forgotten knowledge is supposed to be lived and experienced. But, all of those who teach this make all the excuses in the world for why either they haven't or you can't find it.

It is all nonsense. It is all playing to the minds and the wallets of those on the spiritual path who seek some sort of allusive esotericism that can not be had, except only by the most holy.

But, who is the most holy? Usually those who are dead or those whom you are not allowed to live with and see their flaws.

What is now?

Stop believing the illusion.

You are living the now, right now!

What you are feeling is your now.

When you are hating your job, that is your now.

When you are happy. When you are sad. That is your now.

When you are taking your boring drive to work. That is you now.

When you are making love. That is your now.

When you are doing whatever it is you are doing. That is your now.

Stop trying to make, *"The Now,"* some allusive entity that you have to perform spiritual exercises to find.

This is your now.

What are you going to do with it?

About the Author

Scott Shaw is a prolific author and filmmaker. He is recognized as one of the preeminent Martial Arts Masters of the Western World and is a leading proponent of modern Zen. During his youth he became deeply involved with Eastern Meditative Thought. This guided him to Asia where he has been initiated into Buddhist, Hindu, and Sufi sects. Today, Shaw frequently returns to Asia, documenting obscure aspects of Asian culture in words and on film. He is a frequently featured contributor to Martial and Meditative Art Journals and is the author of numerous books on Zen Buddhism, the Martial Arts, Yoga, Meditation, Social Science, Poetry, and Literature.

Books by Scott Shaw include:

About Peace: A 108 Ways to Be At Peace When Things Are Out of Control
Advanced Taekwondo
Bangkok and the Nights of Drunken Stupor
Cambodian Refugees in Long Beach, California: The Definitive Study
Chi Kung For Beginners
China Deep
Essence: The Zen of Everything
Hapkido: Essays on Self-Defense
Hapkido: The Korean Art of Self Defense
Independent Filmmaking: Secrets of the Craft
Junk: The Backstreets of Bangkok
Last Will and Testament According to the Divine Rite of the Drug Cocaine
L.A.: Tales for the Suburban Side of Hell
Marguerite Duras and Charles Bukowski: The Yin and Yang of Modern Erotic Literature
Mastering Health: The A to Z of Chi Kung
Nirvana in a Nutshell
No Kisses for the Sinner
On the Hard Edge of Hollywood
Sake' in a Glass, Sushi with Your Fingers: Fifteen Minutes in Tokyo
Samurai Zen

Shanghai Whispers Shanghai Screams
Shattered Thoughts
Suicide Slowly
Taekwondo Basics
The Ki Process:
 Korean Secrets for Cultivating
 Dynamic Energy
The Little Book of Yoga Breathing
The Little Book of Zen Mediation
The Most Beautiful Woman in Shanghai
The Passionate Kiss of Illusion
The Screenplays
The Tao of Self Defense
The Warrior is Silent:
 Martial Arts and the Spiritual Path
TKO: A Lost Night in Tokyo
Yoga: The Spiritual Aspects
Zen Buddhism: The Pathway to Nirvana
Zen Filmmaking
Zen in the Blink of an Eye
Zen O'clock: Time to Be
Zen: Tales from the Journey

www.ingramcontent.com/pod-product-compliance
Lightning Source LLC
Chambersburg PA
CBHW071705090426
42738CB00009B/1670